GET WHAT YOU WANT— AND DESERVE!

This is the book that shows you how.

It will help you discover where your feelings of inadequacy come from . . . how to assess your potential and realistically decide in which areas change is desirable . . . how friends and relatives and co-workers can help . . . and how your body conveys your self-image.

Bryna Taubman is a talented and successful journalist who, after more than four years of reporting for the *New York Post,* became a producer-writer of local news at CBS-TV. Her skilled, in-depth treatment of the subject of creative assertiveness makes this a book every woman—no matter how confident and successful—will read with enormous profit.

How to Become an Assertive Woman

Bryna Taubman

PUBLISHED BY POCKET BOOKS NEW YORK

Another *Original* publication of POCKET BOOKS

POCKET BOOKS, a Simon & Schuster division of
GULF & WESTERN CORPORATION
1230 Avenue of the Americas, New York, N.Y. 10020

ISBN: 0-671-41654-5

First Pocket Books printing April, 1976

20 19 18 17 16 15 14 13 12 11 10 9 8

Contents

Introduction   vii

Chapter One: Mislabeling   1
Chapter Two: A Few Basics   15
Chapter Three: Getting the Idea   40
Chapter Four: Those Around You   62
Chapter Five: Outside Help   82
Chapter Six: Getting to Know You   95
Chapter Seven: If I Say That, He'll Die   110
Chapter Eight: Hidden Aggressions   126
Chapter Nine: The Manipulators   132
Chapter Ten: Finding the Words   146
Chapter Eleven: Hating, and Loving, Assertively   164
Chapter Twelve: The New and Different   182
Chapter Thirteen: The Right Time and Place   199

Bibliography   213

Introduction

WHEN I FIRST told friends and co-workers that I was writing a book on assertiveness-training, the most common response was, "Why are you writing about aggression?" In the beginning, I would simply reply, "It's *not* aggression, it's assertion." I was unsure of the difference myself. While interviewing the various people I discuss in the following pages —as well as another dozen or so who provided specific examples, private experiences and personal responses—I was reading many books that had to do with assertiveness-training.

This book, then, is a compendium. The ideas, suggestions, directions and warnings come from a variety of sources. The interviews with therapists are the most important, I think; that's why I've quoted from them directly in many instances. I interviewed people of widely differing philosophies: clinical psychologists and career counselors, feminists and behaviorists, family therapists and experimental psychologists. To their explanations and instructions, I have added the suggestions of other books and observations from my personal experience. I have also included conversations with women who have completed courses in assertiveness-training and the responses of friends who seem to behave assertively in most situations even without training.

Frequently, specific advice from different sources was nearly identical, and in such cases I often combined the thoughts, experiences and words of several different people in a manner that was meant to present the idea in question as clearly as possible. This book contains many suggestions designed to help you clarify your thinking or identify your feelings; in most cases, the words and questions are those the women I spoke with found most helpful. In *all* cases, the material is based on books by and interviews with therapists.

The chapters on self-image and the people around you are examples. In an assertiveness-training group, these topics would be dealt with as women practiced their new behaviors in front of the others present. Since a lone reader does not have such an opportunity to learn new ways of handling a problem, I have tried to make the examples as illuminating as possible.

My own education in assertiveness-training is the result of long conversations with and patient explanations by the following people. They have my heartfelt gratitude and thanks for their cooperation: Janice LaRouche, Janice LaRouche Associates; Penelope Russianoff, Ph.D., Janice La-

Rouche Associates; Judy Gold, People in New Directions; Karen Flug, People in New Directions; Leonard Bachelis, Ph.D., Behavior Therapy Center; Sandy Stark, Adelphi University; Phoebe Prosky, Ackerman Family Institute; Katherine LaPerriere, Ph.D., Ackerman Family Institute; Warren Tryon, Ph.D., Fordham University; Sharon Kirkman, Boyle-Kirkman Associates; Gailann Bruen, Self-Management Institute; Sharon Bermon, Counseling Women, Inc.; Iris Fodor, Ph.D., New York University and Institute of Rational Living; Janet Wolfe, Ph.D., Institute for Rational Living; and Martin Kantor, M.D.

I'd also like to thank those friends and strangers who volunteered their own experiences and feelings but chose to remain anonymous. This book is theirs as much as mine.

—BRYNA TAUBMAN

New York City

Chapter One

Mislabeling

THE TITLE OF this book is "How to Become an Assertive Woman." The subtitle could be "But *not* a Pushy Broad, Castrating Bitch or Aggressive Dame." Assertiveness is *not* aggressiveness. Learning assertive behavior does not include stepping on people's toes, riding roughshod over other's lives, stabbing co-workers in the back or pushing little old ladies out of the way. Acting assertively does not mean insulting friends, offending relatives, ignoring children or leaving a spouse. Being assertive will not make people dislike you, in-laws avoid you, employers fire you or lovers leave you.

Assertiveness is the expression of your own feelings, wants and needs, learning to act on them and having respect for the feelings, wants and needs of those around you. That seems simple, but it's not. Or, at least, most of us find it hard to act that way most of the time. For example, a woman may find it difficult to refuse a date with a man she doesn't want to see. Assertiveness can help. A married woman may have problems telling her husband she wants time for herself. Some women have difficulty when they enter a roomful of strangers. Others cannot refuse a request from a boss, no matter how unreasonable. Still others find it hard to ask questions of doctors, lawyers, or even public employees. Lots of people are intimidated by salesclerks. Many don't complain about faulty merchandise or a bad meal in a restaurant because they are afraid of making a scene. Assertiveness-training can help you handle these situations and almost anything else with tact, goodwill and self-confidence.

Problems of assertiveness are not confined to women, of course.

Many men have difficulty expressing their feelings, especially if those feelings have to do with failure or loss. But, generally, men find it easier to make known their positive needs than women do. That's mostly a matter of social conditioning. Male children are taught to speak up, to go out and fight for what they want. Girls are more often discouraged from similar activities. As a therapist at the Ackerman Family Institute in New York points out: "Little girls are trained not to be assertive from the time you put a pink dress on them and treat them differently from a little blue-panted boy. The touch toward a male baby is different from the touch toward a female baby. It starts there and it goes right through life."

That is not a new insight, but it is a reminder that assertiveness has not been a quality admired in women. However, times are changing and the derogatory labels suggested in the second sentence of this book are heard less often. When they are used, it's usually to describe a woman who makes the earlier stereotypes seem like Clara Milquetoasts. It is only in the past few years that women have begun to learn to speak out for themselves. For many of them, that change came about because of the political and social movements of the mid-1960s. The civil-rights activity, the anti-war demonstrations, the women's- and gay-liberation movements, the demand for consumer protection and the concern about the environment can all be seen as collective assertions, made by large groups of people who began to challenge some of the traditional thoughts, feelings and ways of doing things.

Women are especially sensitive to labels that seem derogatory. Although most of us were told that "sticks and stones may break your bones, but names can never hurt you," it is the names that make us cringe. No one wants to be called a castrater, a ball-breaker or even a pushy dame. But what's pushy about wanting to choose a restaurant?

The Chinese Restaurant Syndrome

Ellen's husband is a Chinese-food addict. Ellen and the kids like Chinese food, too, but not all the time. Occasionally, Ellen or one of the children steered the family toward a different restaurant for a change, and Paul would pull a routine more suited to a two-year-old than a forty-two-year-old. He pouted about the choice, arguing for a steak dinner when everyone else was happy with Italian. He complained about the lighting, squirmed on his seat, put down all the menu choices and picked at his food. Everyone had a miserable time; the next time the family went out, it was chop suey as usual.

One night, as they were getting ready to go out, Ellen spoke up: "I don't want to eat Chinese food tonight. I want to go somewhere else. And I want to enjoy the meal. I don't want to hear complaints about the food or the waiters or the decor. I'm not responsible for those things and I don't want to be blamed for them. I'm going to an Italian restaurant and you can come along if you want to and agree not to make any complaints. The kids can go with whichever of us they choose."

Predictably, both children chose spaghetti over chow mein. After a minute, so did Paul. He restrained his complaints, the family enjoyed the meal and he later told Ellen he hadn't realized how upset she'd been. They agreed they would try a different, non-Chinese restaurant once a month, but would also eat Chinese food.

Ellen's remarks are a good example of assertiveness. She didn't blame Paul. She talked about what she wanted and how she felt. She listed her expectations and gave him several choices. Paul didn't feel threatened or attacked and, while he might not have liked what she said, he really couldn't object to anything. Because she was assertive, a compromise was reached and everyone was happier.

But imagine what would have happened if Ellen had said: "I'm sick and tired of your lousy Chinese restaurants. If the rest of us want to go somewhere else, you make everyone's life miserable. You're so damned selfish. This time I want Italian food and you can like it or lump it. The kids will come with me." Paul would probably have gone off by himself muttering about castrating bitches and nagging wives. And while Ellen ate spaghetti and brooded about the fight, he would nurse his pride with chow mein and swear never to take her out for dinner again.

Or Ellen could have continued being submissive. As usual, they could have gone off to the Chinese restaurant. Ellen and the kids would be miserable, another family outing would be ruined, and Paul would not know why. But the kids would get the message to keep quiet, regardless of their feelings.

Learning assertiveness is learning to ask yourself: "What do I want? What do I need? What do I need to ask for? How can I ask for that without making a demand? How can I make it clear that this is important to me?" Those are easy questions to ask, but difficult to answer. The important word in each question is "I"; in fact, that may be the most important word in assertiveness-training. Getting in touch with that "I" and learning to respond to its needs is what assertiveness is all about.

Sandy Stark, who has been doing assertiveness-training for two years at Adelphi University, describes it as being able to manage the environment. "Men are taught early on that they could manage their environments. Women are taught they have to play with the cards that are dealt them. They don't get to deal; they don't even get to manage the dealing. They've just got to take what they've got and make the best of it. For us to learn that we can manage our environment, manage our relationships, is a very heady thing. It's very exciting."

Control is a very important part of assertiveness. And it is important from the beginning to learn that you *do* have control. You can decide when and where to assert yourself. You can decide which situations are uncomfortable and where you are satisfied with things as they are. Of course, you must also learn to make choices and take responsibility for them. Assertiveness-training is not a guaranteed road to happiness. Once you learn to assert yourself, things do not automatically get better, people do not always do what you want, jobs do not come falling into your lap. However, your chances of getting what you want improve greatly when you let other people *know* what you want.

The Big Bust

Karen and Bob, who have been dating for three months, are remarkably compatible in everything from sex to politics to food. But Bob does one thing that drives Karen wild: he can't resist making leering comments about other women's well-developed breasts, avidly scanning men's magazines for long inspections of the largest, nudest busts on display.

Although Karen has an attractive, firm body, her own breasts are small. In a culture that often equates female sexuality with bust development, Karen finds Bob's attitude both irritating and hurtful.

Yes, he obviously desires her, she tells herself; yes, he often comments on how pretty she looks; yes, yes, yes, but she still can't stand it.

One night, when both are feeling mellow after a good dinner, Karen broaches the subject: "I don't think you realize how much it bothers me when you talk about other women's breasts. We've never spoken of my feelings about my breasts, which I consider small. Because it bothers me, I would really like it if you stopped talking about other women's busts and stopped looking at those nude photos in the magazines, at least when I'm around."

Bob is surprised, then apologetic. It never occurred to him that what he considered casual, half-joking comments upset Karen. Once he realized it, he stopped. He cared too much about her to hurt her.

Lots of women find that assertiveness problems are situational. Some women can express their feelings to their husbands, but not to their bosses. Others can refuse an employer, but not a friend. Still others have difficulty with in-laws, or children or strangers. There are a few women who are comfortable being passive, always responding to the needs of others. They enjoy doing and caring for others. But most people are not happy being totally passive. They feel frustrated and helpless and isolated. They may not know what is wrong or why, and their unhappiness often expresses itself in unexpected ways. For example, inappropriate temper tantrums may hide an assertiveness problem.

That Time of the Month

Joyce works on an engineering journal, the only female editor among a dozen men. Most of the staff treat her with respect, but one old-timer finds her presence in the previously all-male enclave a distinct problem.

Joyce feels he deliberately snubs her, belittles

her abilities and makes every effort to single her out when mistakes occur. Once, when she became angry at an obviously careless error by the magazine's printer, her nemesis commented: "Listen to her carry on! It must be that time of the month."

Because the other men treat her well, Joyce feels she shouldn't pay attention to the lone dissenter. If he wants to act like an idiot let him.

But she's upset nevertheless. She finds herself avoiding the man's office, walking out of her way not to pass it. She finds she's dreading editorial meetings, waiting tensely for him to crack a joke at her expense. If an assignment means working with this man, Joyce's usually sharp editorial abilities evaporate into nervousness.

One day Joyce's nemesis makes a serious mistake himself: he loses ten pages of an important story. It's not a common error, which compounds it, but one that would be ordinarily forgiven in someone who usually functions at an efficient level, such as this man.

Losing the pages means a full weekend of extra work for Joyce. When informed of the mistake, she begins to shriek in rage: "I won't stand for such incompetence. He damn well should be fired. It's time we stopped coddling the stupid fool."

When she calms down, Joyce feels like a stupid fool herself—for losing her temper, for getting hysterical, for facing a problem in an unprofessional way.

Joyce could be helped with assertiveness-training. She could learn to nip a trouble situation when it begins to fester, not to take abusive behavior from others. Had she spoken up, firmly and quietly, when the man first started harassing her, she wouldn't have needed to explode to express her resentment.

Dr. Leonard Bachelis is the director of the Behavior Therapy Center in New York City. He is a licensed psychologist who offers assertiveness-training workshops to men and women. He talks about some of the problems common to both males and females.

" 'Intimidation' is a word I use often, usually to drive home a point about how a person is intimidated by others. Such people are fearful of other people's responses. They worry about how other people are going to judge them, or if they are going to be humiliated or criticized. Some people like being dependent. But there's a payoff for not being assertive. Everything gets wrapped up in being a dependent personality. You have to defer your life to other people. You are in jeopardy in terms of what the other person may or may not do with you. He may abandon you. He may not be benevolent. You certainly can't live your own life if you are dominated or intimidated by others."

Living your own life is a big part of assertiveness. More and more women are beginning to realize that living for others may be comfortable and even pleasant for a while, but it cannot last forever.

Children grow up and leave home. Marriages break up. People die or grow old or move away. Some women need assertiveness-training to break out of the pattern they have accepted without question until now. Others may find the pattern already broken, because the kids are in college or because the family moved or because a marriage ended or a parent or husband died. Facing these situations is very frightening. Things could go wrong. You might make a mistake. What if you can't meet new friends, find new interests? People might get angry or insulted or hurt. You might be blamed for something that isn't your fault. Something new is expected of you, and you do not know how to handle it. That is always threatening.

Women and Work

Dr. Bachelis points out that assertiveness carries over into all areas of life. "Looking for a job requires assertiveness. You sell yourself, in the best sense of that word. You have the freedom to present your talents and your abilities to a prospective employer. You assert yourself by asking the employer questions about the job." Dr. Bachelis further states that many women overreact in work situations, which are among the most difficult for them to face. "The woman who is overly aggressive may feel there is something wrong with her. She may feel she's a dominating bitch. In order to become an executive, she has to be aggressive. That's something that would not be said negatively of a man on an equal rung of the corporate ladder. But, being a woman, people judge her by different standards."

The standards applied to women *are* different, in a bewildering variety of ways. A woman is not expected to take her work seriously. If she does, people wonder what is wrong. They worry about her sex life, her social life, her emotional life. A woman must have better credentials than most men in similar jobs, yet many people still seem surprised to find a highly qualified woman functioning adequately. Women in less responsible positions are often denied advancement. Experienced secretaries watch younger men, and sometimes younger women, become executive assistants—usually at higher pay.

Many of the people teaching assertiveness do so in work-related situations. Sharon Kirkman uses it in the affirmative-action programs she works up for large corporations. Two other women, Judy Gold and Karen Flug, use assertiveness techniques in career workshops for women, workshops designed to help women get more from their jobs. That's a new idea, that women *want* to work and *want* to get something out of it besides a paycheck. Karen Flug says it's part of the women's movement, a process that has made women more aware of the alternatives: "Women need to have more control over their lives and to make individual decisions. They don't have to pick either home or career, but they should be aware that there is a choice and *they* get to decide. I don't think feminism is saying you have to do one or the other. Being a feminist is having the freedom to decide what arena you want to work in and how you want to apply your assertiveness."

Sharon Kirkman has found the same thing in her travels around the country as she talks with women in the corporate suites and factory assembly lines: "It's one of the most positive, exhilarating things that's happening. There are thousands of women who are saying, 'I have really decided I want a career. This is what I want. This is what I want to do' or 'I don't want a career and this is what I want to do.' There are thousands of women who have awakened from a deep sleep and are finally saying, 'A-ha, this is who I am and this is what I want and I'm going to get it. And I'm not going to let anybody hold me back anymore.' I've been working in this area for six years now, and the difference in the mood across the United States is incredible. The most positive thing is there is so much talent out there. More so, I think, than anyone has given credit for."

Feeling Good About Yourself

Learning to put a talent to use is what life is all about. It doesn't matter what the talent is. However, you cannot and will not use it well if you do not feel good about yourself. And that, finally, is what assertiveness-training comes down to: feeling good about yourself, making your own decisions, accepting responsibilities for your choices and making them come true. It is not easy to learn to get in touch with yourself and it may take a longer time until you really get good at it. Even then, you will not be able to do it all the time in all situations. This book will provide you with some help, some signposts along the way, some maps and warnings of the bumps and detours ahead. But, basically, it is a journey that each woman must decide to make for herself. Others can help, give you a push, help you change gears, even carry you for a while. But, eventually, you have to finish by yourself. And that's only half the fun. The other half is when you get there and know it.

Chapter Two

A Few Basics

THE FIRST THING you learn in tennis is the forehand, then the backhand, then the serve. As you get better, you try volleys and lobs, smashes and even trick shots. But, first, you learn the basics. Assertiveness, like tennis, is a skill. If you have difficulty telling your husband when you're angry, your boss when you're upset or your friends when you're busy, this book will help—although, not right away. First, you have to learn the basics.

At Adelphi University, Sandy Stark teaches assertiveness-training to women in the Adult-Education School. She also works as a career counselor and she has found that there is a lot of parallel development: "I've found that as much as I can work with people on decision-making and life-planning, there comes the end of the course, and nothing goes anywhere unless they are assertive." The reverse also holds true. It is impossible to be assertive unless you know what you want—from a husband, a boss, a friend or life in general.

One of the first steps in assertiveness-training is to decide which areas need work—situations where you feel uncomfortable or awkward or out-of-place. Some of the following questions may help you put that into perspective.

In the Family

Do you serve meals whenever someone is hungry, regardless of your own schedule?

Do you chauffeur the kids to all their activities, even when biking or walking is possible?

Do you suggest a restaurant when you all go out?

Do you make suggestions for the movies?

Do you find yourself exploding over minor problems?

Do you have difficulty saying no to your mother? Other relatives? Children? Husband?

How often do you tell your husband, I'm really angry with you? I love you?

How often do you say that to your kids?

How often do you tell your mother (in-law) that you really are busy and don't have time to talk?

Do you cancel your plans when your husband unexpectedly changes his?

Do you change your plans so the kids can do something they want?

If the family decides to go to a football game, do

you admit that you hate football? Or do you suffer silently? Or do you stay home, telling them to go on without you?

Do your kids and husband help around the house?

Do you find yourself serving as a waitress—refilling a coffee cup or getting a glass of water—as well as chief cook and dishwasher?

Are you the detective in the house, able to locate everyone else's lost belongings?"

On the Job

When your boss asks you to stay late and you have an important date, do you stay late or explain about the date?

When was the last time you asked for a raise? A promotion?

Do you like your work? Why? Why not?

Do you seethe when you're asked to make coffee, but do it anyway?

If you work as a secretary, do you do personal chores for your boss (buying presents, sending cards, flowers, etc.)? Do you like doing that? Have you ever refused?

Do you always get stuck with the arrangements for an office party?

Have you suggested new ideas recently?

How long have you been doing the same kind of work?

Do you make all kinds of excuses when you want to leave thirty minutes early, even if it's only once a month?

Do you feel guilty if you take a few extra minutes for lunch?

Do you feel you are working to your full capacity?

Have you ever refused a request from your boss?

Have you ever refused a request from a co-worker?

Do you get upset when someone points out a mistake you made?

Are you afraid of being fired?

Do you get nervous when someone criticizes your work?

In General

Would you complain if you were overcharged at the supermarket?

Have you ever refused a salesman's pitch?

Have you ever sent back a meal in a restaurant?

Would you tell a contractor, superintendent or landlord that repairs to your home or apartment were inadequate and must be redone? Would you do so without yelling?

Have you taken merchandise back to a store

without creating a scene? Did you get a refund or credit?

Do you generally complain about poor service or shoddy merchandise?

If someone pushes in front of you on a line, do you ignore it or tell him off?

If someone is playing a radio too loud, do you ask him to turn it down?

Do you remind people that they are overdue in returning borrowed items?

Do you remind people who have borrowed money from you to repay it?

Can you walk into a party or join a group without feeling anxious?

Do you ever start a conversation with a stranger? At a bus stop? In a bank line? Anywhere?

Do you give to every charity that comes your way?

Do you accept leaflets that are handed out on the streets?

Do you stop to listen when confronted by a sidewalk fanatic?

Are you nervous when dealing with officials? Police? City employees?

Do you tell your doctor when you are angry about being kept waiting?

Do you call your doctor when you feel sick or wait until it's more convenient for him?

Do you get nervous when salespeople criticize your judgment while shopping?

Do you complain if the hairstylist cuts your hair too short?

Do you tell neighbors that their dog (kids, fights) is getting on your nerves?

These questions—and their answers—can give you some idea of areas in your life where you may be having problems. For example, if you find that most of the questions in the family area called for unhappy answers in your daily life, you should concentrate your energies on that. If, on the other hand, you find that the questions about work reveal problems, that's the area needing attention. Whatever part of your life is causing discomfort is the place where assertiveness-training can help. But, remember—you have to learn forehand and backhand before you can try an overhead smash. You have to learn and practice the skills before you can apply them to situations that seem threatening to you.

One of the first steps in assertiveness-training is finding the areas where you need help and deciding which are most and least important. With the help of the questions above and your own feelings, try to list eight or ten situations where you would like to be more assertive. Remember that this means being in touch with your own feelings, but not pushing those feelings onto others. It also means respecting the right of others to have different feelings. Try to list your situations in order, beginning from the least risky to the most involving. For example, your list might be:

1) Salesclerks—I don't need their help in selecting an item.

2) Restaurants—Sending back food without a scene.

3) Doctors—I want to know what's wrong with me and why.

4) Phone—I want to be able to say I'm too busy when I am.

5) Parties—I'm afraid to approach conversations and join in.

6) Boss—I hate staying late when I have something else to do.

7) Kids—I want them to listen without having to shout at them.

8) Husband—I want to know more about family finances.

9) Lover—I want more frequent sex.

10) Mother—I want to see her less often because every meeting is a drag.

That's a fairly wide-ranging list, and is offered only as a guide. Use your own judgment in making your list of problem areas and be especially careful regarding your own feelings about what is risky and what is not. Try to clarify your goal in a sentence so you can keep it easily in mind.

Everyone's list will be different. The problems that seem insurmountable to one woman are not even noticed by another. For example, in *Don't Say Yes When You Want to Say No,* Dr. Herbert Fensterheim and Jean Baer suggest two exercises to help improve assertive behavior. The first is to walk into an uncrowded restaurant or coffee shop and ask for a glass of water. The other is to ask for change of a dollar at a small store. Both situations seem equally impersonal and not very risky, but it all depends on your personal feeling.

To Sandy Stark, an assertive person in most areas of her life, asking for a glass of water sounded risky and she didn't think she really wanted to try that. The second exercise was less threatening to her because it was more personal— she is always asking for change for parking meters. On the other hand, I personally found the water exercise easy because I often do that to take an aspirin. But I do not have a car and rarely ask for change, even for a bus. It was our own experiences and feelings that added an element of risk to two relatively unthreatening situations.

Once you have made your list, you can watch for problems that occur. When they do, especially those at the least risky end of your list, try to remember how you acted. Do not do anything yet but, as soon as possible, write down what you remember about the incident. What were your feelings? What did you say? How did the other person respond? How did you feel? Then what did you say? Go through the whole scene in your mind, trying to remember your feelings and how they changed.

As long as you have a pencil and paper out, here are a couple of other exercises that will help put you in touch with yourself and your feelings, the first step toward assertiveness.

Who Am I? Part I

Write at least ten answers to that question. Use whatever you want to identify yourself as an individual. Keep that list because there will be more on this.

Life Plan

On another piece of paper, write a description of your life ten years from now. Where will you be living? What kind of house will it be? Where are your kids? Your husband? Your current man? What kind of work is he doing? What are you doing? What are your hobbies? Your work? Your interests? Make it as fanciful or as realistic as you choose. Try not to go overboard, like: my husband will be President of the United States and we will live at 1600 Pennsylvania Avenue. But use your fantasies. Have you always dreamed of a house with a swimming pool? A tennis court? A live-in maid? Eight bedrooms? Or a tiny apartment with a terrific view? What do you want ten years from now?

The purpose of this exercise should be obvious. What do you want out of life? That is part of assertiveness-training. Knowing what you want and then going out to get it is crucial.

Now that you know what you want, what are you

doing about getting it? That's the next step. If some of your dreams seem beyond your financial abilities, how can you change that? If you are working as a secretary and see yourself as an executive in ten years, what can you do to make that a reality? It will not just fall into your lap, even with assertiveness-training. You have to be ready to take opportunities as they come. Read, take courses, experiment with what you want.

Activity Log

Still holding that pad of paper? Good. This is a daily exercise beginning right now. Keep it up for a week or so, and even longer if the week is unusual. The idea is to find out how you are using your time. The best way is to make a chart showing how you spend every hour, or half-hour. For example:

7 A.M.: made breakfast for Joe, kids.
8 A.M.: got everyone off to school, work.
9 A.M.: made beds, cleaned up bedrooms.
10 A.M.: talked to Jill, then to Mary about bake sale.
11 A.M.: ran to cleaners, picked up Joe's shoes.
Noon: made lunch for kids, me.
1 P.M.: went shopping for groceries.
2 P.M.: still shopping.
3 P.M.: P.T.A. meeting.
4 P.M.: gave kids a snack, began dinner.
5 P.M.: still making dinner, put in a load of wash.

6 P.M.: dinner, washed the dishes.

7 P.M.: folded laundry while watching news, got after the kids about homework.

8 P.M.: checked on kids' homework, another load of wash.

9 P.M.: started getting kids ready for bed.

10 P.M.: kids asleep, watched television.

Again, that's just a guide. Use your own time and activities, even your own words. After a week or so, look at all the logs together. How much time do you spend on yourself? Do you want more time for yourself? To do what? How can you get it? With a week's worth of logs, you should have a better idea of how you spend your time and in what areas you can take up slack. For example, why can't Joe, in the fictitious log above, pick up the dry cleaning and shoes on his way home from work? Can the kids get their own snacks? Lunch? Make their own beds? Fold their own laundry?

Who Am I? Part II

Let's go back to the "Who Am I?" answers. When Judy Gold and Karen Flug use this exercise on their People in New Directions workshops, they find that most women answer the question in terms of other people. Do you do that? Are your answers of the "I am Mrs. John Jones" or "I am Mary Jones" variety? Do you say, "I am the mother of Linda and Larry," or do you say, "I am the mother of two"? Look at all of your answers. Do any of them really say anything about you, as a person?

Sharon Kirkman interviews women all the time. Mostly, she interviews working women, women in positions of some responsibility in the corporations she designs affirmative-action programs for. Although she tries to get women to talk about themselves, she says: "Women are terribly good at hiding. You ask a woman to define who she is or what she is or describe herself and when she gets done talking, you don't know any more than you did when she started. That's because she defines herself in terms of other people and things. 'I live here. I do that. I'm married. I have children. They do this.' That isn't what you asked."

Look at your list again. Is there anything that defines *you?* Do you like chocolate ice cream? Or walking in the rain? Can you sculpt or sketch? Ride a horse? Read books? Try the exercise again but, this time, give it some thought before you put down answers. Think about your life. What do you like to do? What kind of books do you like to read? Do you prefer some time to yourself or do you always like people around you? Do you have pets, plants, hobbies? What are they? Do you like exercise? Housework? Cooking? Think about yourself, what you do and do not do. Why not? Now try the list again, giving answers about yourself, your life. Make it positive and upbeat and a real description of yourself, the things you like to do that make you an individual.

Compliments

Most unassertive people find it very difficult to be positive about themselves, even when other people are. Women, especially, are very good at putting themselves down, often without meaning to. At a career-counseling workshop at a New York N.O.W. chapter, every woman in the group began with a putdown: "Well, I'm not sure I'm very good at anything . . ." or "I don't compare with the rest of the women here . . ." or "I'm not sure I can do what they want . . ." Further, most women have surprising difficulty in accepting a compliment about anything remotely personal. Despite the traditional view that women are more vain than men, almost all women find it difficult to just say "thank you" when someone notices their promotion, their dress or their house. Some women become very hostile, saying: "Oh, this old thing. I've had it for years. I just dragged it out of the closet." After a response like that, she probably will never get another compliment from that person.

Other women just giggle when confronted with a compliment. That is especially true in job situations. At their workshops, Judy Gold and Karen Flug find that even in a faked interview women with good credentials begin to giggle and deny the appropriateness of their experience. That is non-assertive behavior, reverting to a confused little-girl role, giggling shyly and asking for more reassurance from the interviewer.

One woman told how she had struggled with compliments for years, never knowing what to say. One day she met a friend and commented on her dress. The other woman said, "Thank you." The first woman said: "That just floored me. I just stood there. I couldn't believe it. She made it seem so easy and natural. Just 'thank you.' I decided to do the same thing. And I have ever since. I think I get more compliments this way, too."

It's not easy to set up a situation where you can be sure of getting a compliment; but, if one happens along in the next few days, try saying "thank you" and nothing more. Do not explain where you bought the dress or describe how it looked before you got on the bus this morning. Just say, "Thank you."

To go along with that, try complimenting the people you see regularly. Find something that is new or different about them—something that looks nice, even a haircut or a shoeshine, or a project at work that was well done. Do not say anything unless you really mean it. That is the other side of not accepting compliments graciously—giving ones that do not mean anything. Try to find something you really like, even if it's only, "You look good today," as long as you mean it.

Paying compliments may seem unusual for asertiveness-training, but assertiveness is not all negative. Although most people take assertiveness courses because they have trouble saying no, many forget that the opposite is important also. It is easier to stand up for yourself if people notice you. And people are more inclined to notice you if you have noticed them first. Also, paying compliments is a way of expressing an opinion and taking responsibility for it. That is what assertiveness-training is all about.

Flashing Red Lights

The next exercise is designed to make you more aware of what you are saying. This is not something to change yet, just something to be aware of, some words and phrases that should make flashing red lights go off in your head. Try to remember, note, write down or in some way recall how often and to whom you use the following phrases. Listen to yourself for a week and keep a record.

"I'm sorry, but . . ."
"You may not believe this, but . . ."
"This may seem silly (unimportant), but . . ."
"I've got to be honest (frank, real) with you . . ."
"This is probably not right, but . . ."

There are more, but you get the idea. They are qualifiers and what they qualify is you, your ideas, your opinions, your feelings. Being aware that you use them and when and with whom may make you conscious of assertiveness problems you have not yet thought about. Keep a record of some kind and look for a pattern. When are you least sure of your ground? With whom?

Listening to Yourself

This is another exercise, suggested by Sandy Stark at Adelphi and other assertiveness leaders, to help you listen to yourself and really hear what you say. The idea is simple. Put a tape recorder near the telephone and turn it on every time you pick up the phone. Although it is illegal to record both sides of a conversation without telling the other person, it's perfectly okay to just record yourself. That is all you need. Be sure to mention the name of the other speaker near the beginning of the conversation. That way, when you play it back, you will know whom you were speaking to and probably how you felt. Two or three days of doing this is enough, but do it longer if it seems to be helping. Listen to the tapes after three days of recording but not before. Go into a quiet room and play it all back at the same time. You will be amazed at what you hear, how different you sound when you are bored or busy or interested or in a hurry. You will also hear the hesitations and speech patterns you use.

Learning to Relax

This is probably a good time to start learning relaxation. Many behavior therapists use relaxation techniques because people are more receptive to new ideas and thoughts when they aren't nervous or uptight. Learning to remain cool and calm can help you get through all kinds of difficult situations. Most people become more anxious when they consciously try to relax. It's like trying to make yourself fall asleep. The more you think about sleeping or needing sleep, the more wide-awake you are.

There are books or courses that can teach you to relax. Transcendental meditation, for example, uses a chanting technique. By repeating a single word, usually a nonsense syllable like "Om" or "Ras," other thoughts are excluded and your mind is said to become free of nervous thoughts, allowing your body to relax as well. That is one way and, if it interests you, try it.

Another Eastern method is yoga. That doesn't mean you have to spend a lot of time standing on your head. There are books, courses and even records that use yoga techniques, with or without the exercises. It is important that you find some method you are comfortable with and practice it. Relaxation, like other parts of assertiveness, can be learned, but it takes repetition to learn it well.

Records or courses are very helpful, especially in the beginning. You can listen to someone else and let your mind wander. If necessary, buy a book and read parts into a tape recorder so you can listen without thinking about it. After some practice, you will learn the routine and know in what directions to push your thoughts. As you become familiar with being relaxed, you can recall the mood almost at will. That is what you are aiming for, but don't try to rush it. It will come to you more easily if you just let it happen.

Relaxation is important to assertiveness. It helps you to be more open. If you can consciously relax when you feel panicky or anxious, you will deal with a situation more assertively. Feelings of anxiety and hostility inevitably make you aggressive or compliant. Dr. Penelope Russianoff, a behavior therapist who works with assertiveness-training workshops, explains: "You can't really deal with criticism when you're uptight. Your energies are all going into being tense and tight. If you're really relaxed, you are much more open. If you are backed up with a technique to deal with criticism, you don't have to fall into the standard traps of getting defensive or breaking into tears."

Calm Scene

Sometimes it's difficult to fully relax, especially in the middle of a tense or emotional situation. In her courses at the Self-Management Institute, Gailann Bruen suggests a technique known as the Calm Scene: "With all your senses you envision a place where you had once been really you. This shouldn't be a place really, but an experience where you were really yourself. Using all your senses—sight, sound, everything—recall what you saw, what you smelled. There can be no other people on the scene. There can be groups of people, but nobody that you personally knew, because that could be good or bad, depending on your associations and your vibes about these people. It's important that there be no crutches, no alcohol, no cigarettes. You could have been engaged in minor activity, but nothing strenuous. This is a very good system for achieving a relaxed state of mind. I feel you can't assert yourself unless you're relaxed first."

Vacation scenes are particularly good for this kind of thing. I use a moment from a vacation six years ago as my Calm Scene. It was my first morning in Israel, and I had had about three hours' sleep in the forty-eight hours before that. I woke up very early anyway and went out on the balcony of my hotel. I could see the Mediterranean below me. When I feel nervous, I flash that scene: the sun coming up behind me, the sea in front, the clarity of dawn in a new country. I felt very good and very alive and very self-confident. I use all my senses to bring it back—smelling the sea, listening to trucks make early-morning deliveries, watching the sky change colors, feeling the breeze blowing in from the sea, even tasting the salt air.

By picturing that scene for a few seconds, I can bring back my emotions, the confidence and joy I felt, the freedom and lack of tension. In a few seconds, I feel that way again and can then face whatever is in front of me. When you find your Calm Scene, practice with it. Go back to it again and again. When you feel nervous, close your eyes, take a few deep breaths and bring it back. Use all your senses to recapture the scene. When the picture is firm, try to relive your feelings at the time. Feel the peacefulness and calm take over your body and your mind.

Get Ready, Get Set—Start!

All of these exercises are starting points. It is necessary that you actually do them, not just think about doing them. It is important that you write out your answers to "Who Am I?", that you describe on paper your life ten years from now, that you keep an activity log for a week or two, that you list your assertiveness problems in order. By writing them down, you clarify your thoughts. Some may be things you have never consciously thought about before. The idea is to start *thinking* about those things, start listening to yourself, how you feel, what you want.

The answers to "Who Am I?" should be positive, a list of abilities, interests and qualities that you admire in yourself. Once you have a good list, one that really feels like you (and it may take a few tries), copy it onto a piece of bright-colored paper, such as a sheet from a legal pad. Make several copies. Put one in your purse, one in a drawer you open frequently, one in your medicine cabinet or tucked into the stereo cabinet. When you spot that paper, you will think of the list and of the good things you can do, the person you are, your individual talents and abilities and traits. It will remind you that you are a person with exactly the same rights and privileges as everyone around you.

The life-plan exercise is equally important. The

most successful people set goals for themselves. As they reach one, they set forth to achieve another. Some goals are short-term ones, something to do next week or next month. Others are longer, taking several years to achieve: a salary to reach, an office (political or career) to obtain, a promotion to earn. A few are lifetime objectives, something to spend a whole life working toward—a life-style, a masterpiece. The life plan helps you to clarify your goals, to decide what moves you can make and how long to wait. Look at your plan again. Find a long-range goal, something that will take a few years to do. What do you have to do to achieve it? Can you take a course, read a book, start an activity?

Most women spend only ten to fifteen years of their lives actually caring for children. By the time the kids are seven or eight years old, they are more interested in playing with friends then running home to Mommy after school. Certainly, by the time they are in high school, a mother's constant presence is unnecessary and probably unwanted. If you married at twenty or twenty-five or thirty, you will be forty-five or fifty when the kids are on their own. What will you do with the next twenty or thirty years? Recent studies show that women are more affected than men when the kids leave home. It is called The Empty Nest Syndrome. Mothers are left with little to do. Household chores are reduced, especially if the parents move to a smaller house or apartment. Instead of feeding a family of four or five, there are only two left. Time hangs heavy.

The activity log also helps here. You can begin to make time for yourself to get involved in things that interest you and have some future possibilities as well. One woman in a career workshop run by Judy Gold and Karen Flug kept the log for a week and reported that she had not realized how much of her time was spent doing things for others that they could do for themselves. She had thought she had no time for courses and could only do part-time work at home. When she looked at her log, she realized that she had a lot of time, provided the rest of the family—teen-aged kids and adult husband—did some of their own chores and cleaning. Once she discovered that, she began thinking about working full-time and eventually found a job that worked into her reduced household schedule. Remember that only slightly facetious sociological rule: work expands to fill the time available.

Listing assertiveness problems provides a framework for you, a scaffolding from which to build and add. It is almost impossible to stand up for your rights in a situation with people who are important to you, a husband or parent or boss, until you feel comfortable. Janice LaRouche, who has been doing assertiveness-training for years, used to tell her groups to practice assertiveness on someone unimportant to them, like the butcher. One day, a group member remarked that she had no trouble asserting herself with her husband, but her butcher was a real problem. Make your own list, but begin with the least threatening whether it's your butcher or your husband or the check-out boy at the super-market.

This is a new behavior and it is not easy to learn. It takes time, and you will make mistakes at first, slip toward aggressiveness or turn compliant. By listing problems in order of their riskiness and by concentrating on the easier ones until you gain confidence in your ability to assert yourself, you improve your chances for success in later, more threatening assertions.

Start Small

Georgia worked in an ad agency as a copy-writer for a boss who had the unpleasant habit of handing out last-minute rush assignments. Georgia did her best with these two-second wonders, but her boss always found something to criticize. Georgia knew she could have done much better if she had more time, but was afraid to speak up about the impossible situation. When she took an assertiveness course, her group's first assignment was to test themselves with a small problem. That week, Georgia's boss came in with the usual rush job. Nervously, Georgia blurted out, "You always give me last-minute work. I don't do it as well as I could if I had more time. Then you criticize me and make me feel worse."

Before she had even finished, the boss began

yelling about the importance of this particular assignment and the need to do it super-fast. Georgia went at it and didn't try to say anything else. But, understandably, she felt more pressured than usual. When she went back to her group and reported on the experience, the leader suggested that she go along with her boss for a few more weeks, but try asserting herself in a less risky situation, perhaps with a dry cleaner or cab driver.

The following week, Georgia was reporting about happier incidents. She managed to send back a hamburger that was too rare and had gotten her landlord to fix a leaky faucet. Both situations made her feel a lot more confident; by the end of the course, she was able to face her boss as well.

The point of this story: start small. Don't tackle the most difficult person in your life as the first test of your newly acquired assertiveness. The exercises in this chapter are designed to build beginners' skills only. Later chapters will add bricks to the foundation you are starting to build now.

Most of the exercises in this chapter will take a week or so to do, in order to find a pattern right for you. One day's activity log is not enough. Neither is one taped home conversation or a single day of recalling when you qualified what you said and to whom. *Take the whole week before you go any further*. Do the relaxation exercises every day. Practice your own Calm Scene. Learn to call on that. Go slowly. Do not force anything or, like Georgia, you may fall on your face when you take too large a step. But even if you do, just pick yourself up and take a smaller step next time.

It is probably a good idea to read this whole book slowly, perhaps a chapter a week, as though you were taking a course. Take time to learn each chapter, to think about it, before you read the next one. Try to identify with the examples. Details are not important, but the general ideas are. Did someone ever give you something you didn't want? What did you say? How did you feel? Try to find yourself in each example described here. Imagine how you'd feel, how you'd handle it, what you'd say. Assertiveness-training is education, learning a skill, and it has to be done in small steps, and slowly, if it is to be effective.

Chapter Three
Getting the Idea

EXAMPLES ARE THE best way to learn assertiveness. Most woman don't know how to express their feelings because they have had so few examples to learn from. Even the most talented, skilled and intelligent women are more used to using traditional methods to describe their needs. A woman is accustomed to tailoring behavior to the responses of the people important to her. Some women use tears or cajolery or flirting. Others try nagging or yelling. A few use silence, submerging or ignoring their own feelings. This chapter gives some examples of non-assertive behavior, offers some assertive responses to the same situation, then provides some samples of the right assertive response.

Telephones

Geri works in a small law office with three men, and they all share a researcher and secretary. All four lawyers are supposed to be on an equal level although William, who has been there the longest, hands out cases and checks the work of the other three. The three men always let the telephone ring for a minute before picking it up, so Geri finds she answers the phone a lot. William never answers the phone, which is part of his general attitude of letting others do the dirty work. He also has a habit of yelling across the room to talk to someone instead of going to the person's desk or asking him to come to his.

Most of the time, Geri suffers in silence. She resents taking messages for William, hates being asked to prepare last-minute reports and shakes with fury every time William shouts. But she hasn't said anything because she doesn't want to make a scene.

Geri's actions are perfect examples of passive behavior. In the first place, William may or may not be aware of how angry she is. She cannot be sure until she tells him. As long as she remains silent, he definitely won't change and she will continue to suffer. But Geri is afraid to speak up because she is concerned about the consequences. William might get angry and yell back at her. Or, as he usually does, he might revert to sarcasm, although he's sarcastic even when she doesn't say anything. He has been known to humiliate people in the office for little or no reason and seems to enjoy it. Keeping silent has not stopped him.

After several months, Geri finally loses her temper. She answers one too many phone calls for

William, bangs down the receiver and stalks over to his desk. "I'm sick and tired of answering the phone for you," she begins. "You never do a damn thing except boss people around and humiliate them. You're a bully and a loudmouth. I can't stand the way you shout across the room. You're rude and arrogant, and I'm not going to put up with it anymore."

William has several choices. The most likely one, because he feels threatened and defensive, is to yell back. So a shouting match, with the rest of the office watching, begins. In a few minutes, Geri is put in a position where she must either back down or quit. She can either lose her job or slink back to her desk, more afraid than ever to open her mouth and probably convinced that she will be fired soon anyway. Her temper tantrum has not gained her anything, and William has now reinforced the general resentful atmosphere in the office. The others do not like being bullied either, but it doesn't seem to bother them as much as it does Geri.

There is a third alternative to handling the problem—the assertive way. Geri could answer the phone, hang up and then walk to William's desk. She can stand there quietly and say: "I don't like answering the phone all the time. I've been keeping track and I answer it 90 percent of the time. The other guys do it the rest of the time. You don't seem to pick it up at all, even if no one else is here. So, from now on, I'm not going to take any messages for you. If I answer the phone and it's for you, I will say you're not in and I don't know when you'll return."

William is going to be surprised and angry, but he cannot order Geri to answer the phone for him. In the next few days, he picks up the phone a few times, at least when he's expecting a call. Geri is pleased with the results of her effort and decides to try again. She feels more confident now because William has not yet responded about the phone calls. The next time he shouts at her across the room, she again walks over to his desk and stands quietly.

"I don't like to be shouted at. If you want to talk to me, you can walk across the room, or you can ask me to come here. I'm willing to get up and walk over. But I don't want to be yelled at."

Once again, William says nothing. Geri has told him how she feels and has offered a compromise. She is willing to come to him, so the yelling is unnecessary. In neither case has she directly blamed William's actions for her discomfort. Instead, she takes the blame directly: "I don't like answering the phone all the time" or "I don't like to be shouted at." William doesn't feel threatened and doesn't have to fight back. And that is the heart of assertiveness: expressing your own feelings, taking responsibility for them and letting others know how you feel. Then they are free to make their own decisions about how they want to act.

Not every problem is going to be solved with an assertive response. Sometimes, the other person just does not care how you feel or what you want. Sometimes, your request may go against their own feelings. Here are two examples of unsuccessful assertive behavior.

Doing the Dishes

Barbara and Ted have been living together for three years. They have worked out a satisfactory, share-and-share-alike arrangement about house-work. If Barbara cooks dinner, which she usually does, Ted does the dishes. But Ted does like to cook and, if he has time or Barbara's very busy, he will take over the cooking chores. Then Barbara does the dishes.

One night, Ted cooks. He's leaving the next day on a ten-day trip and Barbara, as she walks into the kitchen, says: "I'd like you to stay and talk to me while I'm washing up. I hate standing here alone to do the dishes and I'd like to have you for company."

Ted stops for a second, then shakes his head. "I want to look at the newspaper. There're only a few dishes, and you'll be done in ten minutes. We'll talk then, when you're through."

Barbara tries again—and again. Ted continues to refuse and they both get more and more irritated. They end up having an argument that lasts long enough for the dishes to be finished. When

Ted leaves the next day, the air still hasn't cleared. What went wrong?

Barbara's first request was assertive. She told Ted what she wanted and even offered an explanation. But that was not what he wanted to do. Instead of respecting his right to spend the time as he chose, Barbara repeated her request. Ted began to feel he was being nagged and became more determined not to give in. Barbara was feeling rejected and wanted Ted to agree to stay as proof he cared more for her than for the newspaper.

At the end, Ted was furious because he'd been manipulated into doing what Barbara wanted— even if it was through an argument. Barbara got what she wanted—company while she did the dishes—but not the way she wanted it. So she still felt rejected and unhappy.

In this case, the assertive request—"I want you to keep me company"—changed to an aggressive demand—"I don't care what you want; I want you to do what I want." Although Barbara didn't attack Ted or blame him, neither did she respect his right to spend his time as he wished. That is the other half of assertiveness. It is necessary not only to know your own wants, but also to realize that other people's needs may differ from yours. Recognizing the rights of others to do as they wish is as important in assertive behavior as being able to say what you want to do. If you cannot allow others the freedom you wish for yourself, assertive behavior becomes aggressive and usually unrewarding.

Bikes and Buses

Molly lives in New York City and although she rides her bike everywhere, she must travel through city streets and worries about the wild careenings of the buses and cabs that share the roads with her. They often cut her off without warning, pushing her into the curb, or pretend to try to hit her. Molly has talked with other bikers and knows it's not just her imaginaton; there are drivers who don't like bike riders and menace them on city streets.

One afternoon, Molly was riding her bike peacefully when a bus came up from behind, swerving so close that she went into the curb and lost her balance. The bus stopped for a red light, and Molly went up to the driver's window.

"I don't think you were very nice. You almost killed me and it wasn't necessary to come that close. You should have more respect for people's lives, especially if you are a public employee." The driver started to laugh, and Molly lost her temper, yelling and cursing at him. The light changed and the bus pulled away, managing to run over Molly's bike and nearly hitting Molly as well.

Molly was shaken and upset. She knew she'd been rude, but it was the bus driver's fault. He shouldn't have laughed at her. She was frightened and angry and decided never again to speak up to bus or cabdriver or anyone else in a car when she was on her bicycle. She picked up her ruined bike and shakily made her way home.

The problem here was not what Molly had said, but what she'd expected to happen. She wanted the driver to say: "Gee, lady, it's really nice of you to take such a pleasant tone after I tried to kill you. I'm sorry. If I'd known you were such a sweet lady, I wouldn't have done it." Of course, that did not happen. In fact, the driver didn't even acknowledge how civilly and assertively Molly had approached him.

It does not help to be assertive in some situations. Total strangers don't care how you feel. Cabdrivers may slow down if you ask them, but then they may not. Just because someone is unappreciative of your assertiveness is no reason to feel the assertion was a mistake. It may not have worked; however, that doesn't make assertive responses wrong.

It's important to recognize that there are some places and people where assertiveness is not possible. A later chapter will deal with some of these cases and discuss alternatives. For the moment, it is necessary to understand that assertiveness, even though it's done correctly, may not win you the response you want. Once you understand that, it becomes much easier to respond without getting angry. Molly's reaction to the bus driver's laughter was anger mixed with resentment. She wanted him to be aware of and admire her courage and ability to confront him. He couldn't care less about either, and that made her furious.

Her decision to never again confront bus drivers and similar people is a copout. There may be times when assertiveness will be more rewarding. It will probably be effective to ask a cabdriver to slow down by saying: "I don't like to go this fast. I'm not in that much of a hurry and I would like you to drive more slowly." If the driver doesn't do so, you can add: "If you don't slow down, I won't tip you." However, most cabbies will drive more slowly if asked.

More Buses

June had a different kind of unpleasant experience with a bus driver. She had pulled the bell string to alert the driver that she wanted to get off at the next stop. Although the bus was halfway across a busy intersection, the man stopped and began yelling at June. "What's the matter, lady? Can't you wait a minute? You want to get off right here in the middle of traffic? I'll let you off when I'm good and ready and I don't need anybody ringing bells all the time."

June experienced a few seconds of anger and fear. Why was he yelling at her? What had she done? She had simply signaled her desire to get off at the next stop. Then she realized the driver had his own problems and was taking them out on her, even if she wasn't personally responsible. So she just smiled and said: "I'm sorry you got that impression. I only wanted to let you know that I wanted to get off at the next stop."

The bus moved off and, without a word, the driver opened the doors at the stop. June got off, feeling quite pleased with herself. She had not responded to the driver's remarks in an argument she could not possibly win. Nor had she contributed further to the scene. Instead, she had repeated her request firmly, ignoring his outburst and allowing him to cool down without embarrassment.

June was successful because she didn't get angry. She realized the man was not attacking her personally, so she just repeated her original request. Janice LaRouche, who teaches assertiveness-training to women in the New York area, calls that keeping on your assertive center. The idea was developed by her colleague, Dr. Penelope Russianoff, and the image has been helpful to many women who have learned assertiveness from them.

"It's the right to be me," Janice LaRouche explains. "It has to do with a basic definition of an assertive person. She stands up for her rights, her feelings and opinions and her right to those feelings and opinions. When you've been thrown off your assertive center, you may concede all that because you are unable to do it. The assertive person is armed with the knowledge that she is perfectly able to say to somebody: 'I don't agree with you. This is what

I believe.' You may choose or not choose to say that but, when you're thrown off your assertive center, you can't do it. It's a very uncomfortable feeling. You feel manipulated."

Your Assertiveness Center

Dr. Russianoff uses a concrete image to explain the assertive center. It is an imaginary core of security that goes through your body, through the spine. You stand straight because your spine and your core of security are straight. When you are thrown off it, you cringe back. That's submissive behavior. Or you can step forward to meet the attack. That's aggressive behavior. In both cases, you lose that inner core of security. An assertive person would take a step back during the attack, move to center and respond without anger. Stepping backward, mentally or physically, allows you to give a little.

The assertive center is like a palm tree: it sways under a strong wind, then returns to its original position when the pressure ends. To change the image, it's like catching a bat. If it's a hard fastball, you have to give a little with your hands and go with the motion of the ball to ease the impact. Once you've caught it, you can return to your center position.

Janice LaRouche remembers the first time Dr. Russianoff's concept helped her. "I used it when I started to get angry. It was very helpful. I just caught people's manipulations, put them aside and went back to my nice core of security. I have a perfect right to my place in the line no matter what people are throwing at me: 'You're stupid. You must be in an awful hurry, blah, blah, blah.' I just kept thinking, I guess he doesn't like my looks or something. I just stood there. I really had the physical sensation of being centered, with my feet on the ground, my back straight and my assertive chant well prepared and ready to repeat: 'This is my place in the line and the end of the line is over there.' "

The assertive chant is a concept that will be treated in another chapter but, basically, it is an expression of your rights in the face of opposition. In a precious case, Barbara had tried it with the dishes, but the situation was inappropriate. In the case of a person trying to get ahead of you on a line, the assertive chant is more effective. It also works with uncooperative salespeople when you're returning merchandise or requesting a refund.

It Didn't Get Clean

Susy divided her wash load very simply. Shirts and blouses went to the Chinese hand laundry. Linens, towels, underwear, pajamas, jeans and the like went to a service laundry, where the dirty clothes were washed, dried and folded, but not ironed. The rest, sweaters, suits, dresses, tablecloths, wools and linens, went to the dry cleaner. Susy tried to make friends with the nearest dry cleaner wherever she lived. They cashed checks for her on weekends, took in packages if she wasn't home, waved as she waited for a bus in the morning.

One day Susy took her good lace tablecloth along with a couple of pairs of slacks to be cleaned. When she picked them up, she noticed that all were hanging in plastic bags. Usually, the tablecloth was folded and wrapped in brown paper. A couple of weeks later, Susy got the tablecloth out for a dinner party and saw that the wine and coffee stains from the last party were still there. So was the cleaning ticket. She decided to take the tablecloth back.

Susy explained to the cleaner that it had apparently been cleaned wrong because the stains that normally came out were still there. She thought, perhaps, it had been dry-cleaned instead of laundered.

"We send everything to the same place. I don't know what could have happened," the cleaner said.

"I would like to have it laundered, but I don't think it's right that I should pay for it. It should have been laundered the first time and then it would have been clean."

The cleaner disagreed. "I don't know that those stains will ever come out. If you want to have it laundered, you'll have to pay for it. I can't be responsible if you order the wrong kind of cleaning."

Susy tried again. "I've brought this tablecloth in before, and you always sent it to the laundry. I don't think I ever tell you where to send it. This time, by mistake, it was dry-cleaned, and I paid for that. But it's still dirty, so I want it laundered and I don't think I should have to pay for the mistake. I'm a regular customer. I thought of you as a friend and I can't believe you want to save the money at the expense of a friendly customer."

The man gave in, and Susy left, feeling much better. She had been able to settle the problem without an argument. The next morning, she waved from the bus stop, to show she was still friends. When she picked up the tablecloth, the stains were gone, without charge.

That was a good assertive chant, one that responded to the other person and still conveyed the message. Susy was not blaming or accusing the dry cleaner. She pointed out that a mistake had been made and what could be done to fix it. His hesitancy was overcome when Susy reminded him of their usual good relations. She answered his arguments calmly and repeated her assertion: a mistake had been made, and she wanted it fixed. Susy and the dry cleaner were both happy with the ending.

Assertive chants work best in situations where you are protecting your rights against the encroachments of others. It doesn't work, as Barbara discovered, when your rights threaten the rights of someone else. And it can be a problem in an intimate relationship; the chant can turn into a nag. It is most useful when someone is trying to manipulate you.

We Never See You

For ten years, Margie lived in New York City, working happily in advertising, living by herself, seeing lots of friends. Her parents lived in Detroit and worried about her constantly but since they didn't like New York and Margie's apartment was small, they rarely visited. Usually, when they came East, they stayed with Margie's brother, who taught at Yale, in Connecticut. At first, Margie managed to see her parents every time they visited, even if it meant changing her own plans. However, as she got more and more involved with people and things in New York, that became more difficult and she occasionally missed a visit.

At one point, in May, a block party was planned, with Margie as chairperson. She'd rush home from her job to spend another six hours planning and organizing. There were all kinds of arrangements to make, from food and chairs to publicity and entertainment. Margie arranged for a fire engine to come by, for the police to block off the street and for a PuppetMobile from the Parks Department.

When the phone rang on a Tuesday night, Margie wondered what new crisis was approaching. It was her mother, wanting her to come to New Haven that weekend. Margie explained she was busy.

"You haven't come up to see us the last couple of

times," her mother complained. "We miss you terribly. We were really hoping you could find the time for us this time."

Margie repeated her first comment with a further explanation. "This weekend is impossible, Mom. I'm chairperson of the block party, and there's loads to do. I would like to see you, but this weekend is out."

That did not seem to get through. Margie's mother tried again: "This is the last chance we'll have to see you until next fall. Dad and I are leaving for Europe and won't be back until the end of September. If you don't come this weekend, it will be almost a year since we last saw you."

Margie repeated her chant: "This weekend is impossible. I have too much work to do and it's very important to me to do that work. I would like to see you, but this weekend is out. Perhaps we can find a time when we are both free and can spend a lot of time together."

Margie's mother tried guilt next: "You care more about your new friends than you do about your family. If you really loved us, you'd find a way. But I can see that you don't want to. I don't know why you don't like us anymore."

Margie was beginning to get really upset, but managed to remember her chant. "Although I'm sorry you feel that way, I still can't make it this time." She repeated the litany about her work load, suggesting an alternate date for a get-together before her parents' trip.

Finally, her mother gave up. She reluctantly acknowledged that Margie would not be coming to New Haven, but had promised to call before the trip.

Margie hung up the phone feeling very pleased with herself. She had made it clear that this particular weekend was inconvenient and she had not allowed herself to be manipulated. It was not the first time she'd refused her mother, but it was the first time she'd done so without argument and bitterness.

Although the assertive chant was one of the secrets of Margie's success, there were others. Margie softened the blow by her repeated reassurance that she *did* want to see her mother, but not that weekend. Not even the guilt trip laid on her—"You like your friends more than Mom, who bore you and cared for you. After all we've done for you, you're refusing one little request! You're selfish and heartless"—changed Margie's mind.

Empathy is an important part of assertiveness. Showing consideration for other people's feelings is part of recognizing their right to have them. But empathy can be carried too far. Women are especially prone to what the authors of *The Assertive Woman* call the Compassion Trap. Having been taught from earliest childhood to Be Nice and "Do unto others as you would have them do unto you," many women are afraid to show their negative feelings. Instead, they try all kinds of tricks and silent communication to get the message across.

I'd Rather Not, Thank You

Linda met Franz at a party. He was German, working for a while in his company's American offices. He asked for her phone number and, although she didn't want to see him again, she couldn't think of a nice way to refuse. How could she hurt the feelings of a pleasant stranger to her country? So she gave it to him.

He called two days later, and Linda tried to get away quickly. She said she was just leaving, would he call again. When he did, she used still another excuse, but promised to call him back. Naturally, she didn't; so, in three days, he called once more.

Desperate, Linda tried more direct tactics. "Franz, I'm really sorry, but I don't want to go out with you. You're wasting your time by calling."

"What's the matter? Don't you like me? I thought you wanted me to call."

Linda was nervous, yet stuck to her point. "I enjoyed meeting you at the party, but I don't want to see you again. I guess you're just not my type. I shouldn't have given you my phone number because I knew I didn't want to go out with you. I'm sorry you wasted your time."

But Franz didn't want to give up. "What do you mean, I'm not your type? If you like talking to me, why won't you see me again? Is it something I did or said? What is it?"

Linda repeated, "I don't want to go out with you. I can't quite explain it, but I just don't think I'd be comfortable with you. We're too different. I'm sorry I misled you. Good-bye." Feeling very tense, she hung up before he could reply.

This problem situation cropped up because Linda wanted to be too nice. She didn't want to hurt Franz's feelings by refusing to give him her phone number. Had she refused honestly at the party, she could have avoided the later problems. Instead, she was "nice" and opened the door to more complications.

She made another mistake when Franz called the first time. She said she was too busy to talk and he should call back, expecting Franz to realize he'd been brushed off. However, he didn't realize this. So he called again, and Linda greeted him with warmth, this time promising to call him. She figured (hoped) if she never returned his call, he would learn—in a "nice" way—that she wasn't interested.

Linda never realized some important facts. The only behavior you can change is your own. The only emotions you can control are your own. You cannot be responsible for other people's reactions to something you say. Lastly, most people are a lot stronger than the rest of us think. Rejection is never pleasant, but most people get over it.

Franz would have been much less hurt if Linda had refused his request from the beginning. Turning down a stranger—or getting turned down—is difficult enough. Refusing someone you know well—and hearing "no" from a friend, relative or in-law—is ten times more difficult. But, if you are very clear about what you are refusing and why, it can be handled without anger or resentment by either party.

We Don't Want Anything More

Sarah and Dick had been married about a year, very happily. They both worked at jobs they liked with promises of good futures. And both liked the casual way they were furnishing their apartment, mostly with castoffs until they could find a really special thing they wanted. But Dick's mother was horrified with their life-style. She sent them presents —paid-for and delivered—beginning with kitchen equipment, blenders and mixers, pots and dishes, then moving through the rest of the house. Packages came filled with tablecloths and matching napkins. Or towels and sheets. Then she sent a bridge set. A lamp. Pictures.

Sarah and Dick tried to hint that the gifts were out-of-place and too expensive, but she answered their objections with: "They'll fit in as soon as the rest of the place is furnished. You two really need a couch and a coffee table." Sarah felt pushed into a corner of her own house. The items were nice, but not her taste. She didn't want to hurt her mother-in-law's feelings, yet something had to be done. The next time Dick's mother called, Sarah decided she'd had enough.

"Mom, it's really nice of you to send these presents. I know how much you enjoy doing it. It makes Dick and me feel good to know that you do so much for us. We know how much you love us and we love you, too. But most of the things you've sent us we don't need. There are some things we do need and want; so the next time you feel like sending some things, please call me first. That way, you can get us something you know we need and will enjoy getting. However, I want you to know that we'll love you just as much even if you don't buy as many presents."

Sarah's mother-in-law was silent for a few minutes. Then she said she hadn't realized how they felt and would certainly call before she bought anything else. The next time she came over, Sarah and Dick mentioned a bookcase they were thinking of getting. Dick asked his mother if she would pay for part of it because they couldn't swing the entire amount themselves. She agreed. From then on, she bought only presents they wanted.

Close friends and relatives usually survive rejections, especially if they are handled as nicely as Sarah's. In many cases, the problem situation has been accepted for a while to spare the other person's feelings. When a refusal is finally made and an explanation given, the hurt comes not because of the rejection itself but, more frequently, as a result of the earlier acceptance of the problem. When a newly assertive woman refuses to do something she always used to do, the most common response is: "Why didn't you tell me before you didn't want to do it?" Husbands, kids, friends, relatives and even bosses are insulted not basically by the refusal, but by the lack of trust and honesty expressed when the woman agreed earlier to something she knew full well she didn't want.

Chapter Four

Those Around You

THIS CHAPTER IS like a box of candy—the more you pass it around, the less weight you gain. This chapter suggests some of the ways you may find yourself changing and the effects of those changes on the people around you. That is not to say that the changes are bad, but they will make you different. You will not always respond the same way to requests or take the easiest way out. For example, you will assertively protest being short-changed at the supermarket the next time that happens. Then, instead of feeling angry for letting yourself be taken without speaking up, you will feel more positive about yourself and your financial abilities. In turn, that could lead you to take a more active interest in the family budget.

If you do the exercises and assignments prompted by this book, you will change some of your ideas and your outlook, and the people around you have to notice those changes. It's only fair to explain why those changes are happening and how else they may affect you. It would be grand if those near and dear could help and support your efforts, but that may not happen. After all, your new behavior may make life uncomfortable for them for a while. Few people voluntarily undergo discomfort for long.

The title of this book implies a certain dissatisfaction with the way you are presently. If you have read this far, some of the situations are familiar and the solutions welcome. You are probably uncomfortable with your current reactions to life and would like to find a happier way of meeting difficulties. So you want to change. But change can mean discomfort.

Coping with Change

Many things change all the time: the weather and the government, your weight and appearance, your feelings and behavior. Children grow and change. Parents grow old and increasingly helpless. Spouses leave or die or become incapacitated. Families move. Jobs are lost. Accidents occur. Assertiveness-training can help you to take changes in stride, both the changes you make within yourself and the changes forced on you.

However, change remains uncomfortable, and most people resent external changes in their lives. If you are changing internally, that may help you, although it will probably create changes in your relationships with the people around you. Depending on you and them, the effect can be good or bad. But first you must recognize and face it realistically.

Because assertiveness-training concerns getting

in touch with your feelings and learning to express and act on them, try to decide exactly why you are reading this book. What situations make you uncomfortable? Which people seem to inhibit you? What would you like to happen when you assert yourself? What changes do you want to make? How do you want people to act? How much of a hardship would that be for them? How can you best indicate the changes that will help them as well as you? Write out your answers to these questions and go over them. How many of the situations on your assertiveness list involve people you see regularly— spouse, lover, children, parents, boss, co-workers, friends? How will the changes you want affect them? Let's take a specific example.

If you have been the kind of woman who never chose a restaurant or movie and your husband has gradually stopped asking you, he would be understandably surprised if you suddenly rejected his choice. He might even resent you for speaking out, no matter how pleasantly and assertively you opposed his suggestion. Or he might feel betrayed, thinking that for years you went along with his choices when you really didn't like them. Mostly, he would be confused. Why are you suddenly expressing this opinion? What was so wrong with *this* choice that you were forced into speaking out?

Obviously, the more compliant your previous behavior, the more uncomfortable changes will be for the people around you. If you considerately, but inconveniently for you, kept hot food ready for, whenever the various members of your family decided to eat, they will be quite put out when they learn you want to stop doing that. Or suppose you always pick through the clothes on the floor of your daughter's room, taking the dirty ones to the laundry. No matter how much you nag or threaten, she never gets around to cleaning up herself. But, if you decide to stop, close the door and walk away, she will soon find herself with only dirty, wrinkled clothes. And she probably won't be very happy about it.

"You're Not the Woman I Married"

In her assertiveness-training courses at Adelphi, Sandy Stark has found that many women experienced resentment when they tried to assert themselves with family or friends. But Ms. Stark says there are ways to meet that. "One person in a household changing the rules all of a sudden is a very traumatic thing. You've been in a relationship with your husband for twenty years and, all of a sudden, you change the rules. He legitimately says: 'You're not the woman I married.' "

To lessen the surprise and perhaps gain some help and understanding, try to talk with the people around you who will be affected. This doesn't mean long, intimate chats with co-workers or bosses. It can be done as situations arise by making it clear what your limits are. With families, though, things are different. It's easy for a boss to support your changes if he gives you the promotion you request, because, it's to his benefit to do so. It is not necessarily as obvious to your family that cleaning up after themselves instead of relying on you will prove equally good for them. But that is frequently true.

Janice LaRouche has been doing assertiveness-training and career-counseling for women for several years. "People act very differently toward a woman who is learning assertiveness. Some just hate it and want nothing to do with her. Others dislike the compliant or aggressive behavior that preceded it, so they are delighted with the change. Still others hate the short-range effects, but learn there is a long-range benefit they never anticipated."

Ms. LaRouche offered the example of a woman who refused her widowed mother's annual vacation visit, explaining that the family had decided to stay at a dude ranch that summer. For a while, the older woman resented her daughter, accusing her of selfishness and heartlessness. But, finally, Mother decided to do something and took herself off to Florida with some friends. They had a great time, especially Mother. The long-range results were much happier than expected. The daughter's family had a good time at the dude ranch, Mother had a good time in Florida and they all enjoyed her next visit a lot more.

Two Vital Truths

Remember, assertiveness-training teaches two main points:

1) The only behavior you can control is your own.
2) People are not mind readers.

As you learn these two truths and act accordingly, you will soon find that you would like others to be equally aware of them. Your change and growth will be better if those around you are also changing. But that may not happen. As we've said before, you cannot control other people's behavior, only your own. As Dr. Katherine LaPerriere at the Ackerman Family Institute points out about changing: "It depends on age, age and all the things that go to modify where one is in the course of social development. My guess is that young people would find it absolutely okay. Young men would be willing to listen, willing to read, willing to experiment. With older ones, it really depends on how old the mind of the man is."

Sharon Kirkman recalls a middle-aged executive who had taken part in her affirmative-action program at his firm. Part of the Boyle-Kirkman procedure is to spend a day with the male executives, talking to them about their feelings and prejudices about women. When she returned a year later as part of the follow-up program, Ms. Kirkman found this man troubled. "I still feel uncomfortable. When I have to take a business trip with a woman, I very honestly feel uncomfortable—not because she isn't good, not because she isn't capable, not because she isn't a total businesswoman. It's just that I can't change everything I've always thought about women. I'm forty-five years old. I've thought about women only one way and I can't, overnight, think about them differently."

It is difficult to change yourself. Demanding that

others make changes to keep pace may be asking for trouble and failure. Instead of demanding that your family and friends change their behavior to fit your new needs, try moving more slowly and with more preparation. They will be more likely to take one step at a time than to climb a mountain in one leap. And you will be more likely to reach the top of the mountain, or any other goal you set, if you don't have to push them ahead of you.

Money, Money, Money

The easiest way to get someone to do something is to show them that it would help them as well as you to do it. Let's take an example. If you, like most women, know little about the family finances —how much the mortgage is and how long, how much insurance you all have and what it covers, even how much money is in the checking account —it may be unpleasant if you suddenly confront your husband, determined to know more. He will wonder at your sudden interest, possibly even remind you of times past when you wrote bad checks or could not balance the checkbook. You may eventually learn what you want, but you will probably face a lot of anger first.

There are other approaches. You could suggest that it might be a good idea for you to learn about these things, in case he is injured or ill. You could point out that if you knew more about family finances, you might be more careful about your spending. Finally, you could gently remind him that accidents do happen and, if you were suddenly left alone, you would have to learn these things anyway, probably under very difficult circumstances. · Given those reasons, your husband probably would agree to help you understand the insurance policies, mortgage conditions and other matters of personal finance. Or he might not. You can then accept his refusal and decide your next move.

Assertiveness is not easy and it doesn't always work. There are some people who just don't want to do things your way. There are others who see any remark by any woman as aggressive and unnecessary. If you live with someone who cannot bear to be refused or opposed, assertiveness will not help you when you confront his problems. But then you can decide whether you want to continue living with someone who is so selfish and inconsiderate.

Fortunately, few people are that bad. In most families, love and concern for one another are paramount. Any opposition others show to your new behavior may not really reject you as you now are but as you were.

More Coffee, Dear?

Darlene and Bob have been married for twenty years. Like millions of others, she cares for the house and family, and Bob goes to work each day. Although she likes cooking and cleaning, there are some assumptions about her role that Darlene doesn't like. There is Bob's expectation that she should wait on him whenever he needs a refill of food or drink. He never specifically asks her to do this; he just expects it. And Darlene has never refused or thought about refusing. It just bugs her every time it happens.

One evening, Bob's sister was visiting. As usual, when Bob finished his coffee, he gently waved the cup, his signal to Darlene that she should get more. However, this time she refused:

"If you want more coffee, it's in the kitchen on the stove. I don't like it when you wave your cup at me and expect me to wait on you. Why should I get up instead of you?"

Bob was surprised, but went to the kitchen, carrying his cup. The two women heard him mutter, "I wasn't *waving* my cup." A few hours later, Bob reintroduced the subject to his sister while Darlene was out of the room.

"I don't wave my cup or expect her to wait on me. I can get coffee for myself. I don't *wave* my cup like that."

Bob's sister disagreed, adding that she had noticed his habit over the years. It had always made her mad to see Darlene wait on him so casually and she was delighted to hear Darlene speak her mind.

Bob, looking a bit hurt, said, "Why didn't she tell me before?"

That is not an uncommon reaction of husbands, bosses, friends. Your new assertiveness need not be threatening to the people around you. If you take the time and trouble to explain, to talk about their problems as well as your own, it probably will not be. But it will be uncomfortable, and the only way to ease that is with practice.

Support is helpful. Now that Bob knows that Darlene doesn't like to wait on him, he can respond in several ways. Since he already said he doesn't mind waiting on himself, he can try not to ask her so frequently. And when he slips and does ask, he can try not to resent it when she says no. If they both forget, whoever recalls first can point it out, with as much goodwill and humor as possible.

Speak Up!

People are not mind readers. They cannot know what you want until you tell them. In light of your previous behavior, your new wants may seem unrealistic or unnatural to them. In that case, an explanation may be in order. Let's go back to the daughter's dirty room. If you have spent the last few years yelling, arguing and nagging about the mess, try ignoring it for a while, Then call the teen-ager and say: "I don't like nagging you about your room. Anyway, it doesn't seem to help. I end up picking my way through books and clothes to get your dirty laundry every week and I just get more furious. So I'm not going to do that anymore. From now on, if you want clean clothes, you will have to throw the dirty ones in the hamper. If you want pressed clothes, you will have to hang them up or iron them yourself. You are responsible for your clothes, and I will no longer bug you about them."

At first this may be hard. And you may occasionally find yourself wandering through the room, picking up dirty underwear. But, just because you do it once doesn't mean you have to keep doing it. If you go a week the first time, try to make it ten days before checking in the next time. Or two weeks. It will not take too long for the supply of underwear and clean clothes to run out. Then it is up to your daughter to do something about it herself. It may prove uncomfortable for a while. After all, putting dirty clothes in a hamper or carrying them to the laundry room is hard work, right? Sure. A teen-ager or even a younger child is certainly capable of caring for his or her own clothing. It may seem unfair to your daughter not to have clean clothes without effort and not to have a maid to clean up after her; but who said life was fair?

It is possible to get the rest of the family to go along with you. Keep in mind the two basic premises of assertiveness: You can control your own behavior. And, there are no mind readers. Follow these to their logical conclusions. Sometimes it helps to understand how the other person feels. Remember, you cannot read minds either. You may have to ask a few questions before you learn the truth.

For example, in the incident cited a few pages ago, if Bob had acted unhappy after Darlene refused to get him coffee, she could have asked what was wrong. And Bob might have said: "The coffee thing is really bothering me." Darlene could then assume that he didn't like waiting on himself and resolve never to mention the subject again. Or she could ask: "Why?" And then Bob would probably say to her, as he did to his sister: "Why didn't you say something to me before?"

Your Man May Feel Betrayed

This is another aspect of the assertiveness problem that often comes up in family situations. Many men feel betrayed when their wives begin to act differently. They think, "If she loved me, why didn't she tell me what was bothering her? I would have helped. Why does she have to go to a book or a course or workshop to get help? Why doesn't she trust me? What is she telling them about me? They must think I'm a fool."

That kind of thinking may seem silly; but, in a later chapter, you will learn how you do the same thing. Right now, however, let's concentrate on your husband or lover. Does he feel this way? Ask him. Talk to him about it. What does he think happens in your group? Or what does he think is happening in your head? What is he afraid will happen? There are lots of women's lib scare stories around, about women who wake up one day and decide they want a divorce or a new life or an exotic job. Maybe he's afraid you will leave him. Or maybe even gentle assertions threaten his image of himself. Sandy Stark has found that many men are unhappy when their wives begin to change. "A lot of

women make different decisions—to go back to
school or to go to work or to run their lives differently. And that becomes very threatening and uncomfortable for the man around her. He is used to
supporting her. He likes supporting her. It makes
him feel important. Now she is saying she wants
to contribute and this is important to her. All of a
sudden he is very uncomfortable. His masculinity
feels threatened. He's had all these years of other
stuff, and he cannot be expected to turn around
and say: 'Terrific!' Much as he may recognize that
in his head, his stomach is saying a whole different
thing."

With time and tact and assertiveness, you can
change his stomach's reaction. In Janice La-
Rouche's groups, she suggests that the women
adopt some of her own personal reactions. "I tend
to see other people as benefiting from my assertiveness. I think I'm more predictable, and they are less
responsible for me, which is a great burden off
their shoulders. I simplify their lives by making my
own decisions, not being so easily manipulated.
They're no longer respon ible for what I do, which
should be a great relief to them."

Learning to Take a Risk

Responsibility is a large part of assertiveness. By
learning to know what you want and telling others
and working for it yourself, you take some of the
responsibility of succeeding or failing. You may not
succeed if you try. You certainly won't succeed if

you don't try. Assertiveness is taking that risk. If, for years, you've been going along with others' choices of restaurants and movies, ask yourself why. Do you really not care what and where you eat or what you watch? Or are you afraid that someone else may not like your choice?

If you suggest a restaurant and the food is bad, are you really responsible for the way the chef cooks? If the movie is terrible, is it really your fault? Or is it just a mistake, and your next choice may be terrific? Many people don't assert themselves because they don't want responsibility. But there are few situations where your entire life can succeed or fail on one decision, and I can guarantee it will not be what movie to go see. If you go to a bad movie or restaurant once, you can always go to a different one the next time. If you don't get one job, you can keep trying for another one, perhaps a better one. If much of your life is spent being afraid to tell others what you want to do, you cannot get much of what you want.

Some women are afraid of assertiveness because of the changes it will bring. It could make their husbands unhappy, their bosses angry and their friends upset. It could. But it probably will not. Janice LaRouche has found an answer for that, too. "That's a chance you take, but you also take a chance by remaining the person you were. There's very little guarantee that you're going to cement someone to you by any behavior pattern. And if you want to devote your life to finding the right behavior pattern to keep someone glued to you, hop to it."

Why Shouldn't a Man Wash His Own Socks?

Ms. LaRouche's associate, Dr. Penelope Russianoff, suggests a different approach: "Modern women are challenging the messages that culture has been giving them. They are challenging these questions and beginning to realize that they should know about family finances and legal problems. They should know where the jewels are and if a second income would help. It is hard for a man or even a child to realize that as a woman changes and challenges the cultural-historical explanations with which she has been raised, her man and child might benefit by challenging, in a parallel way, some of the assumptions with which they've been raised. For example, why shouldn't a man know how to wash out his socks, or thread a needle, or cry? What's so wrong with those things? And if you've got a wife or mother who's got guts enough to grow, then the men and children could consider it an opportunity to look at some of the crazy messages they've been getting and challenge them."

In a similar way, Dr. LaPerriere suggests that husbands are often as dependent on wives as wives are on husbands. It's just more acceptable to note a woman's dependency for income and emotional security on a man, and less acceptable to comment on a man's apparent helplessness with laundry, food and other daily necessities. Dr. LaPerriere says, "I'd be curious to trace that—to see, perhaps, that men simply transfer a lot of their dependency behavior from their mothers to their wives and never get into an adult position at home. It isn't that this is bad; I think we all need some of that. The bad thing is that women don't do it in the same way, in a manner that lets them stay adults with a concept of self."

What's Not Okay

Let's think about that. It's okay for a woman to be dependent on a man for love and money. Society says this is to be expected and that dependency proves a woman is still a child with emotional hang-ups. It is also okay for a man to be dependent on a woman for love—that is not childlike or emotional. But many men are also dependent on a woman to do their laundry, cook their meals and generally clean up after them—just like Momma did. Society has generally ignored the childlike behavior of men. Somehow it is perfectly logical that an adult man has never learned to keep his clothes and belongings in order, except in the army. And if he did it there, why can't he do it at home? Why should it be okay for him to start dropping things on the floor when he acquires a wife?

It is not okay, especially if it bothers you. It is even less okay for you to begin nagging him for not doing things after so many years of a particular behavior. Dr. LaPerriere points out: "When you start unbalancing the pattern of a marriage, you've got to expect some waves."

Her colleague at the Ackerman Family Institute, Phoebe Prosky, agrees: "You can't dictate co-operation. People tend to be taught to see that they've been dominated and beat down, not taught to see that they've accepted it, for whatever reasons. And acceptance has to be given equal responsibility with the perpetrator. If a woman wants to begin to change things, for her to dictate that someone is going to be cooperative is contradictory. And for her to think that, in one moment, she's going to say what she wants and is going to change the family is, I think, arrogant and aggressive in the worst sense. She should realize that she had put herself in that situation, and she will have to assume full responsibility for moving into a more desirable and comfortable situation."

If the man in your life has been dropping his socks on the floor for twenty years, don't suddenly start nagging him to pick them up. He will probable not do it and may instead resent both the nagging and the fact that you are not doing it anymore. Approaching the problem slowly and assertively will probably prove more useful.

If the dirty socks really bother you, talk to him about them. He may not know how much you dislike it—remember, he cannot read your mind—and will probably agree to take care of the socks himself when he learns. If you meet resistance, you could, as we explained in the incident with the teen-ager, present a clear set of alternatives. You do not want to and will no longer pick up his dirty socks. If he wants them washed, he can put them in the hamper himself. Otherwise, he will not have clean socks. If that doesn't appeal to you—you may really hate the sight of the clothes piled on the floor and you do have to live in the room, too —you might offer a compromise. If he picks up the socks, you'll do something he dislikes to do— put out the garbage or clean up after the cat. Or you may dislike doing those things more than you dislike picking up dirty socks. You can decide to pick up after your husband as long as he takes out the garbage and cleans up after the cat.

Janice LaRouche explains that everyone has the right to change the rules of a situation. "If the other person doesn't want to come along, he also has the right to make other choices. You have to be prepared for the implication that your choice means you are a new person, which means giving others the choice of whether they want to be with the new person. It seems reasonable to me, and that's a chance you take."

Few situations are such strong either/or propositions. More often, a newly assertive woman learns that the people around her are pleased with the changes. Your husband may not like having to choose a restaurant all the time. If you offer your ideas, he may want to go out more frequently, knowing that the success of the evening is no longer his total responsibility. Or he may just be glad to hear you say something for yourself.

An Apple a Day . . .

A marriage counselor relates the problems of a couple she was treating: "They were in their late forties or early fifties. He was a businessman, not particularly into psychology. His wife thought she was making herself very clear to him, letting him know her needs. But he didn't even know they were being expressed. We played it through in therapy one day, and it turned out it would have been difficult for anyone to understand what she was saying. For example, he went into the kitchen and came back with an apple. As he bit into it, she asked, 'Is the apple good?' He said, 'Yes,' and finished it. What she really meant, she said later, was: 'Is that apple good? If so, I would like a piece or even another apple for myself.' People come from different coding systems. Often what they say simply doesn't get across."

To repeat again—people do not read minds. If you want an apple, you have to ask for it, or get it yourself. Learning assertiveness is learning to ask for the apple. That can be difficult if you are more accustomed to taking what comes by chance. The businessman above would probably have been only too willing to get his wife the apple if she had asked for it directly. He was certainly more surprised and resentful when she became angry at his lack of understanding than he would have been had she asked him to do her the favor.

Some women find their families supportive at

first as they experiment with assertiveness. That support sometimes fades as the woman becomes more sure of herself and uses assertive techniques more frequently. One reason is the discomfort her new behavior creates. That doesn't mean you should go back to your old ways, especially if you are asking for things you really want. And, sometimes, the problem is not with the others, but with you. Sandy Stark has noticed that when people begin to become assertive, "There's a real rush, a real excitement. There's a real 'I want to assert morning, noon and night' that can drive the people around you nuts."

Assertiveness is acting on your own feelings and allowing the rights of others to act on their feelings. It does not include accusing, blaming or reminding others of past mistakes, but taking whatever action is necessary to improve things now and in the future. If you and your family keep this in mind and treat the problems that come up with humor and not with bitterness, assertiveness-training can bring about changes that will benefit everyone and make everyone more satisfied.

Chapter Five
Outside Help

SUPPORT FROM YOUR family is very helpful as
you learn to be assertive but, for reasons already
explained, it may not always be forthcoming. Outside help is more likely and possibly even more
useful. The problem is where and how to find it.
Friends are one possibility and can be very helpful with some assertiveness problems, yet may not
be supportive when you are asserting yourself with
them.

It is possible to learn assertiveness by yourself,
with the help of a book and some support from outside; however, a group will make it easier, more
fun and less confusing. Almost everyone who
teaches assertiveness-training uses group workshops or clinics. Dr. Leonard Bachelis of the Behavior Therapy Center explains that "groups are
a big help in providing models of appropriate behavior. And they are particularly helpful in giving
reinforcement to people who are learning to be-

come assertive as well as in giving feedback, picking up cues on how assertively or unassertively a person has behaved."

For women, especially, the presence of other women and their reaction, to what is being said and done seems helpful. The group can be used to build your self-confidence. Gailann Bruen begins her assertiveness groups at Morris County College in New Jersey with several exercises designed to help everyone overcome the initial nervousness and insecurity. For example, she has the group break into pairs. One person in each twosome spends a minute or so telling the other something positive about herself, something she is proud of doing. The other person listens silently, then repeats what was said until the first person is satisfied. The two switch roles and, when both have talked, listened and repeated, they join another pair and introduce each other, using the positive information.

"I start with this positive thing because I think it is extremely important, particularly for women. Assertiveness is not a problem for women only, since most of us have been taught not to blow our horns, to be modest. But women have been especially encouraged to support other people, to be sensitive to them, to intuit others so much they don't even know what their own needs are," says Ms. Bruen.

Positive reinforcement is also a factor in the groups run by Karen Flug and Judy Gold at People in New Directions. "Working with a group, people tend to be more objective. Other people, who don't know them, who don't have any friendship at stake at the very beginning, say, 'Wow, you can do so many things.' Another common trend we found is other women always see other people as having more than they have, more qualities, more qualifications. 'But you're so talented and look at me,'" explains Ms. Gold.

So groups can be useful in helping you project a new image of yourself, taking pride in your accomplishments without fear of immodesty. And groups are helpful in other ways, as Dr. Bachelis indicates. They provide role models, feedback, responses to what you are doing. This is particularly important in assertiveness-training for women.

Support from Other Women

"One of the problems with women is that when they start being assertive, they see themselves as being aggressive, as being a bitch or castrater or witch. And men often say that to them. Even when they are not objectively being this way, that will totally turn off the behavior. And this is where the group is so good about giving feedback: 'Gee, you didn't sound like a bitch to me. That sounded pretty good.' And the women support one another," says Dr. Iris Fodor, who teaches assertiveness-training at the Institute for Rational Living.

Gailann Bruen has had similar experiences. "With some of my groups, the women all thought they were being aggressive, but what really came out is that they were not. They were so busy worrying about being perceived as aggressive and pushy broads that they were bending over backwards. No matter what they said, they thought it was aggressive until they got feedback from the group. Most of them said their problem was not submissiveness, but aggressiveness. When we role-played and they got feedback from the group, a lot of the things they thought were aggressive weren't aggressive at all."

You Are Not Alone

Having other people involved in learning assertiveness helps you lose some of your self-consciousness about it. As everyone talks about her problems and risks, you begin to understand that yours are not unique, nor do they seem so threatening. Everyone's idea of risk is different. If you cannot confront your boss, but have no trouble facing up to your mother, there will probably be someone in the group who is terrified of her mother yet feels very secure in work situations. As you listen to each other, both threats diminish.

From her experience with leading assertiveness groups at Adelphi University, Sandy Stark explains: "It goes back to my risk is not your risk. And if we start judging each other's risks, we are being not only *not* helpful to each other, we are damaging each other. I cannot judge what is a risk for you. My risk is not yours and we cannot judge; we can only appreciate each other's risks. Look out for them and point out to each other when we think we are acting dumb and say, 'Look, I think you're being a little crazy about this.' We can do that for each other, but we can't say, 'That is really ridiculous. How could you do such a stupid thing?'"

There are some problems in setting up leaderless groups; it is wise to take them into consideration before you call in five friends to begin your own assertiveness-training. Dr. Bachelis offers some outlines of what an assertiveness group should and should not do: "It's not therapy. People should not get involved with intricate psychological problems. Just stay with the task and be supportive. You've got to help the other person. You might tell her you're angry or that she's not coming across but, basically, it should be done in a context of helping the other person. Don't get your own personal problems entwined with others. Concentrate on a task orientation rather than getting too involved with how you feel about each other and that kind of thing."

Friends

Similar warnings are advanced by Katherine LaPerriere of the Ackerman Family Institute: "If it includes issues that friends share, yes, include friends. If you want to be assertive with friends, then get the friends in. However, if you want to be assertive with your husband, then don't bring in friends. That just invites trouble. That invites issues of broken trust and confidences, especially in a small community. That doesn't make sense."

The point of an assertiveness group is not to find your underlying psychological problems, if any, nor to reveal the intimate secrets of your family life. The group members should be helping one another to get in touch with themselves. They should be supportive and helpful, offering constructive criticism and positive reinforcement. Groups are not helpful if members spend the time criticizing one another's words and actions without offering any way to solve the problem. The advantage of a group is having other people around who can make suggestions and offer help. This is particularly useful in assertiveness-training where someone else who is not threatened by your situation can often see an escape route hidden by your fears.

It's Up to You

Dr. Fodor offers an example from an assertiveness group she was training. "One of the women was unemployed and just sitting at home, waiting for an employment agency to call her. She was just sitting there. She mentioned that she had problems going on interviews and everyone said: 'You have to go down there. They won't come to you.' She lived alone and had very few friends and, when she came to the group the next week, there were a whole bunch of people who were waiting for her. She was the center of attention and she almost *had* to bring something. She talked about her experiences and was very discouraged and depressed because when she went to the employment agency, they told her there weren't many jobs. Although they gave her a few leads, she didn't think they were worth pursuing. The group gave her a lot of support and said, 'Next week, go on one of those interviews.' By the end of the workshop, she had a job. People became involved in helping her; in the process, they all saw their own passive, dependent sides."

Almost everyone involved with assertiveness-training has at least one similar story. The group members support, encourage and get involved with one another, even when they begin as strangers. In their People in New Directions workshops, Karen Flug and Judy Gold have found the group support to be very helpful: "You have a dozen other non-subjective people saying, 'You don't need to take that. Look at all the talents you have.' People are always impressed by others, by having this whole supportive group behind them."

Groups offer more than support, important as that may be. They provide an opportunity to experiment, to test your assertiveness in role-playing situations, to learn from the responses of the group and to try again. The question of what is assertive, aggressive or compliant behavior is discussed and analyzed. Each person can offer her own situation and get the group's impressions. Often, as mentioned earlier, what you think is aggressive, is not.

Man-Woman Assertiveness

Dr. Fodor, who teaches assertiveness to both all-women and mixed groups, offers an example. "A woman starts asserting herself, say, in a role-playing situation with a man. When it's all over, she says, 'I feel so pushy.' Then I ask the man, 'How did you feel?' And he says, 'You know, the last time she was a mouse and I could walk all over her. But, this time, I experienced her as a real person, and it was a real pleasure to sort of know this person.' Then I go around the room and ask, 'How did you experience her?' And it goes around the room and they say, 'You weren't pushy. You were terrific.' What she considered pushy and awful and mean now gets put into: 'Hey, people like that behavior. It's not bad.' "

Role-Play

Practice, through role-play, is an important, technique in learning assertive behavior. It can be done by yourself with a tape recorder, with a friend who is uninvolved in the situation and willing to help, or in a group. If the rest of the group is also learning assertiveness, they will probably be more sympathetic to your failures and more positive about your successes.

Most people who have not tried role-playing think it self-conscious and artificial. It is true that many people are nervous and unsure of themselves when they begin in a role-playing situation, but that usually disappears as each person gets into the matter at hand. Role-playing is easy. You pick a situation on your assertiveness list and practice dealing with it, usually with another person. If you aren't in a group, you might call a friend and ask her to help out with something that is particularly threatening to you.

For example, you might be facing an important job interview and are unsure of how you will act. Call a friend and ask her to play the interviewer. Do it several times with her, responding in different ways each time. Once she can be sympathetic and interested in hiring you. The next time, she might be uninterested in your qualifications. The third time she might be undecided or abrupt. Switch roles. You play the interviewer, and she plays you. Listen to how she responds to your questions and how she acts. Do it with a tape recorder and play it back. Talk about it. Ask her for her reactions. Did you sound interested in the job? Able to handle it? What made you nervous, hesitant, unsure of yourself? Go back and do it again until you feel comfortable with all the possible responses.

You can do that with almost any assertiveness problem, from getting the right cut of meat from the butcher to telling your mother that you will not be able to come home for the holidays. With a group, you can listen to other people's problems, observe how they handle a situation and try it out yourself if it seems right for you.

Chair-Switching

There are other practice techniques that are also helpful. Try chair-switching, a variation of role-playing. If you want to ask your boss for a promotion or your husband for an increase in your household allowance, take their part. Try to think of how they will answer, what are all the possible responses they could make. Then have your replies ready. Part of assertiveness is not allowing yourself to be thrown off-center, not being taken by surprise. That is difficult but, if you practice what you want to say and think about all the arguments against it, you can provide some protection for yourself.

Contracts

Finally, groups are most helpful in making contracts. Sandy Stark explains: "The thing that I have found most useful in my assertiveness-training workshops is contracts among members. That's the thing that does it. Suppose the contractor is a college student who says, 'I'm going to tell my room-mate that I'm tired of her dropping my blouses, which she's borrowed, on the floor. I want them returned to my closet.' She makes a deal. Once you affirm publicly what you want to do, it's amazing what happens. She makes the deal on Wednesday and doesn't do a thing about it for a week. Tuesday night she becomes aware of the fact that the group is meeting on Wednesday, and she has made this contract. She chases her room-mate down so she doesn't have to come back to the group and say, 'I didn't do it.' Affirming something publicly is a lot different from saying to yourself, 'I'm really going to do this.' "

Outside support, then, is helpful in learning assertiveness. It can be from a member of your family, even a child, if he or she is willing to cooperate. Or it may be a friend, if she is not part of your problem. Or it can be a group.

The group can be one you organize yourself, with neighbors, acquaintances, even strangers. Have everyone read books on assertiveness-training while you are together. Try to meet once a week for two or three months so you will have time to work on situations at all levels. Use the group for practicing specific situations that you will have to face. Or bring up something from the past that you would have liked to handle better and try to work out how to be assertive in such a situation.

Groups Without Leaders

Be sure to remember the warnings about groups without leaders. Unless you find someone who knows how to run a group and who's had experience with assertiveness-training, set up rules ahead of time:

- No revelations of intimate details of personal relationships.
- Stick to a specific problem: how to ask for a raise; how to say no to a salesman; what to say to your mother when she invites herself for the weekend; how to suggest to your husband that you would like him to share in the housework.
- Don't get into personalities, but try to give the other members of the group some idea of how the other person would respond. For example, if you're an only child, your mother lives several hundred miles away, is widowed, retired, and hasn't seen you in six months, give the group those facts. Then they will have a better idea of how your mother might respond to your refusal for a visit.

Gailann Bruen provides some rules for her groups when they begin role-playing: "What I do is insist that everyone be positive and say what she liked about what someone else did. Describe what you see and what you hear. React only to what you see and what you hear. Be specific about it. Some people feel very pressured about this and, if they haven't got anything to say, it's better not to speak at all. Because, otherwise, it sounds phony."

If the group seems to be getting away from the point, be assertive! Remind them that you are there for assertiveness practice, not psychological analysis. Everyone should know the rules and feel free to speak out when someone is not following them.

If someone feels put down by that, talk it out. But try not to get into personalities and problems. Assertiveness is learning how you feel and being able to tell others, not analyzing *why* you feel that way or talking about your childhood.

There are assertiveness courses being offered almost everywhere. You might want to find one in your area and go to an organized group. Several Y.W.C.A. branches and N.O.W. chapters have courses in assertiveness-training. Feel free to check out the credentials of the leader and, if you don't like the way a group is being run, leave. If the Y or N.O.W. group near you doesn't offer assertiveness-training, try behavior-therapy institutes, universities or career workshops. The Seattle N.O.W. chapter has published a booklet on assertiveness-training, which offers some useful tips for setting up and running your own group.

If you cannot find a group and do not want to set one up, you can always try assertiveness-training by yourself. Practice with a tape recorder; find a friend, relative or co-worker who can help with specific problems. You can even use a pencil and paper, writing out your problem, the other person's response and your reply. Talk to yourself in a mirror and listen to what you are saying. The important thing is to practice and repeat until you feel sure of yourself and your ability to handle a situation.

Chapter Six
Getting to Know You

ASSERTIVENESS HAS BEEN defined as knowing what you want, being able to tell others about it and being able to work toward getting it for yourself. With that goes respecting others' rights to have different wants from you. But right now, we are concerned with you. You can't be assertive if you don't know what you want. That was explained in chapter two, which also offered some suggestions about how to get in touch with your feelings, needs and wants.

More important, perhaps, is to find out who you are. Chapter Two had included the "Who Am I?" questionnaire. You may have found it difficult to come up with ten positive identifying statements about yourself. Most people do, as a result of our social conditioning that it's not "nice" to be proud of yourself or what you have accomplished.

Karen Flug of People in New Directions puts it another way: "A lot of the problem is a lack of clarity about who you think you are and who you want to be. If you're not sure of your own identity, then all you can do is react to other people's statements about yourself. If you have conflicts about what you want to do, what skills you have and what your expertise is, then, of course, you are going to pull back into yourself and say, 'He may be right.' "

What Are Your Rights?

Assertiveness is learning not to put yourself down. The next chapter suggests some of the irrational beliefs we all use to do that. This chapter offers some ideas to help you gain a better, more positive image of yourself. To begin with, think of your "Who Am I?" list. Take it out and look at it. It should help you have a sense of yourself as a person, as an individual with the same rights and feelings as everyone else, and the same right to express them.

Behind any assertion is the conviction that you have a right to what you think, feel or believe, to express your opinions and disagree with others' reactions. One of the first books on assertiveness-training was *Your Perfect Right* by Drs. Robert Alberti and Michael Emmons. As an appendix to the book, the authors include the Universal Declaration of Human Rights adopted by the General Assembly of the United Nations. The thirty articles list a whole series of rights guaranteed to every human being—including you. Most of these are political rights, so psychologists have developed a list of rights that are more attuned to personal needs.

Patricia Jakubowski-Spector, one of the first behavior therapists to apply assertiveness-training to the needs of women, has drawn up a list of basic human rights:

Everyone, man or woman, has the
- Right to refuse requests without having to feel guilty or selfish.
- Right to feel and express anger.
- Right to feel and express a healthy competitiveness and achievement drive.
- Right to strive for self-actualization through whatever ethical channels one's talents and interests find natural.
- Right to use one's judgment in deciding which needs are the most important for one to meet.
- Right to make mistakes.
- Right to have one's opinions given the same respect and consideration that other people's opinions are given.
- Right to be treated as a capable human adult and not patronized.
- Right to have one's needs be as important as the needs of other people.
- Right to be independent.

You may choose not to exercise all or even one of these rights at any given time. You can exercise some of them some of the time or all of them all of the time. It is your decision, not one that can be forced on you by someone else. Some people who teach assertiveness-training suggest that you use the phrase "my perfect right" whenever you are confronted with an assertiveness problem. For instance, when someone pushes in front of you in line, you say to yourself: "I have a right to my place in line. He does not have the right to force himself ahead of me. He should go back to the end of the line." Then repeat it aloud.

Go back to the Jakubowski-Spector list of rights. How many of them are new to you? Did it ever occur to you that you *could* make mistakes? That you do not have to feel guilty or peculiar for doing something foolish? Or that you must decide for yourself what is important to you? How can anyone else possibly know how you feel about something? Look at the rest of the list. Think about it. Try to recall situations where you could have used one or more of these points. It is important to accept these rights as yours, as part of your social, emotional and psychological system just as the Bill of Rights to the United States Constitution is part of your political system.

Knowing What You Want

Lack of a good self-image is not uncommon among even the most successful and talented women. Gailann Bruen teaches one-day assertiveness workshops for women's groups and has found that almost all the women she speaks with have the same problem. "I did a six-hour workshop for Professional Women in Radio and Television. These were all well-qualified, talented, successful women. What did I hear? 'I don't know what I want. I don't know what I like.' This is tragic. A lot of these women have been home for a long time, but I've had women with their own companies, several who were real-estate brokers, some in pharmaceutical houses. Not the kind of women, you would think, who need assertiveness-training.

If you want to be assertive, to have some control over your life, you have to stop putting yourself down and belittling your abilities. Keep your "Who Am I? list in places where you can see it when you begin to feel down. Look for ways to feel better about yourself and don't be ashamed to acknowledge when you have done something worthwhile. The compliment exercise suggested in chapter two is part of this. Many women brush off compliments with putdowns or belittling remarks: "That old thing." "Thanks, but I thought I looked awful today." "Do you *really* like it?" Besides putting yourself down, these comments insult the giver of the compliment. Yes, he likes it or he wouldn't have said so, even if it is an outfit dragged from the bottom of your closet. If you don't feel your best that day, relax and accept the complimenter's judgment.

In their career workshops, Judy Gold and Karen Flug have found that even highly experienced and talented women become giggly when complimented on their work. If someone tells you you've done a good job and you begin to laugh, what does that tell the other person? Think about it. If you continually brush off or belittle compliments, how many more do you think you will get?

A Sense of Impending Disaster

Can you change how you think about yourself? The psychologists and behavior therapists say you can. One of the best books on this subject is *A New Guide to Rational Living* by Drs. Albert Ellis and Robert Harper. It explains how people convince themselves of impending disaster. The authors believe you can, with some effort, learn to stop thinking that way and instead convince yourself of the new possibilities open to you.

Phoebe Prosky, a therapist at the Ackerman Family Institute, explains it somewhat differently: "If you begin to see yourself as a person who gets what she wants, you have a much better chance. I think there are a lot of intangibles there. If I can change my self-image from a person who does not get what she wants to a person who does get what she wants, by some process I'm going to get what *I* want. I believe, absolutely, that we create our realities."

You Are Good—Believe It!

That may sound a lot like positive thinking and, to some extent, there are similarities. But assertiveness goes a lot further. If you think of yourself as incapable and worthless you will act that way. Soon, others will think of you that way also. If, instead, you look at your list of "Who Am I?" answers to think of yourself as an individual with some very interesting abilities and interests, so will other people. The problem is how to do that.

To begin with, stop making belittling comments about yourself. If the dinner gets burned, apologize, but don't go into long-winded explanations or a self-pitying: "I don't know why this always happens to me." Probably, it does not, so why say that it does? You have a perfect right to make a mistake, one every hour if you choose. That doesn't mean that you're going to keep making the same mistakes for the rest of your life. If you begin to think that way, stop. Go back and remember all the good dinners you have cooked, all the successful meals you have served, and forget about the one that burned.

As an individual with her own needs and feelings, you have as much right to express your opinion as anyone around you. Remember the list of qualifiers in chapter two? How often have you used them? Under what circumstances? Who were you talking with and about what? Why did you feel what you said was silly, unimportant or unnecessary? Were you really right? Did the other person know more about the subject than you did? Why did you feel you should speak up at all?

Building a positive self-image isn't easy and it takes time and effort. Whenever you hear or think of putting yourself down, try to go back and think more positively. Make it a conscious effort. Keep a piece of paper that says, "You are a good person and nice to be around," in your wallet. Write "I feel good" on the bathroom mirror so you can see it first thing in the morning. Give yourself a pat on the back *whenever you do or say* something you are proud of. Think "That's one for me" when something good happens.

If you have a close friend, talk to her. Go over the things you find unlikable about yourself and get her reaction. You will probably learn that the things that seem so awful to you are minor problems to her. You don't like animals, so what? Or you don't like to talk to oafs. Who does? Or you get angry when someone yells at you. We all do. Whatever your faults, your friend's image of your positive qualities is probably a lot higher than of your negative ones, or she would not be your friend.

Try to get in touch with your feelings and what is behind them. Why do you feel so bad about yourself? Many of us are still listening to the critics of our childhood. But now you are twenty or thirty or forty or fifty years old and you are no longer the person that child was. You are wiser and know more about the world. Those criticisms cannot possibly apply to you anymore.

Confront the Past

Janice LaRouche, who now teaches assertiveness, first had to learn to be assertive herself. "Everybody's vulnerable in different areas. If you grew up in a family like mine, where what you did in public was important, you could assert yourself more easily with your family than with outsiders. The important thing was how people saw us—company manners. So I could always yell at everybody in the family with the greatest of ease, but I was very polite outside. I couldn't assert myself at all."

In her courses, Ms. LaRouche sometimes suggests that women who have difficulty asserting themselves find some childhood situation where they would have liked to speak up. They role-play that situation in the group. For many women, confronting that childhood menace is enough to stop the shadow of criticism that has plagued them into adulthood. If that is what's bothering you, you might try the same thing yourself, having a friend play the role of mother, friend, teacher or whoever is your personal ogre.

Whatever is behind your negative self-image, one of the best ways to overcome it is to take some positive steps to change it. First of all, recognize your rights as a person. Read the Declaration of Human Rights, the Bill of Rights or anything else that makes you feel like an individual.

Body Language

Then look at yourself in the mirror. Are you standing straight? Do you slump or lean? When you talk to people, do you look straight at them or do your eyes wander all over the room? Body language and eye contact play an important role in assertiveness. They help convey the impression that you believe in yourself and in what you are saying.

Next, try to imagine yourself in an assertive situation. How do you sit or stand? What do you do with your hands? Is your voice hesitant? Soft? Whispery? Do you stumble over words? This is where practice comes in. If you have practiced what you want to say, it will be a lot easier to remember when the time comes. Talk into a tape recorder and play it back. Is your voice loud enough? Can you be heard clearly?

Dr. Leonard Bachelis uses a rating scale based on voice tone, eye contact, gestures, body language, head position and other physical aspects. "The non-assertive body attitude is deadness, no motion, no life, no emotional expression, no amplitude of the voice, no freedom of the body—in a sense, contracting from the world as opposed to moving out."

In experiments at Fordham University, Dr. Warren Tryon tested what kinds of physical actions add or detract from assertiveness. The experiment was very simple—two actors with a script already worked out. One played a customer in a restaurant who ordered coffee with cream and got black coffee. The other played the waiter. They did the same scene several times, changing gestures, loudness of voice, hesitation of response and stress on syllables. The scenes were shown to college students who were asked to rate the scenes on a continuing scale, with submissive behavior at the bottom, assertive behavior in the middle and aggressive behavior at the top.

"What we generally found was that each of these physical differences was very important to the subjects in their ratings. That is to say, as a person spoke more loudly, he was seen as more aggressive. As people spoke with more hesitation, they were seen as submissive," Dr. Tryon reports.

Dynamic You

When you role-play situations with a friend, ask her to check your posture, where you look and how you speak. Do you have nervous gestures—twisting your hands or playing with a ring or necklace? With time and practice, you can learn to stop those habits and present a more forceful, dynamic and self-assured appearance. One of the secrets of successful assertive behavior is believing in yourself and your right to whatever you are saying. If you don't look like you believe that, the person you're talking with probably won't accept it either.

The Victim Mentality

If you project an image of insecurity or hesitancy, you're asking the other person to take advantage of you. If you're unsure about what you want, others will be even more unsure about giving it to you. Many women have a "victim mentality," believing things happen *to* them. Of course, things do happen to you; events are often beyond your control. But you can control how you respond and what you do afterwards.

Double Messages

Beware of "double messages," when you speak. Remember Linda, and Franz, the date she did not want? Linda was giving a double message each time he called. When she answered the phone, she would say, "Hi. How are you? Nice of you to call." Her voice was soft and friendly; not unnaturally, Franz thought she meant what she said. When she finally explained that she didn't want to see him, he was understandably confused.

Women often don't make their tone of voice correspond with their thoughts and feelings. If you don't want to talk with someone, say so. You don't have to sound abrupt or angry. But neither should you sound as though you really do want to talk. Other "double messages" include a fixed smile when you really aren't happy or an avoidance rather than an outright refusal. Assertiveness is saying how you feel; a "double message," confuses the person you're speaking with. It makes him wonder if you really mean what you are saying.

Gailann Bruen finds double messages all the time in her therapy and workshop sessions: "The same thing can be assertive or aggressive, depending on how you say it. It's not the words. Many times you're saying one thing, and there's no matching; there are no congruences with the nonverbal things you are doing."

Blue Days

Everybody has days when they just don't want to get out of bed. Most of us get up anyway and try to ignore the bad feelings. That can be a problem. Sandy Stark points out: "Women with families, particularly, act as if everything is always okay. They really don't want to show how bad they feel. They deny their feelings, they stuff them and, later, there's a huge explosion when someone drops a napkin."

Inappropriate explosions are only one result of ignoring your bad days. If you ignore how you feel on those "blue days" and try to function as though nothing were wrong, you may find yourself making a lot of mistakes. After you have made a few, you begin to feel you can do nothing right. You are incapable and worthless, and the problems you are having are further proof of this. And that makes you feel even worse. You may feel better the next day, but the memory of those strong negative feelings lingers. Some women even expect to have bad days as a result of their lack of faith in themselves.

Family therapist Phoebe Prosky says: "A lot of people are dealing with an *image* of themselves, rather than themselves. And if their image is that they are good and kind and giving, which is one of the ways you are *supposed* to be, it precludes their saying no."

If you feel lousy one day, say so. That doesn't mean going around the house or office complaining and moping. It does mean that you don't have to

107

be your usual lovable, cheerful self if that is a major effort. You have a right to feel anger or anything else, and you don't have to pretend you aren't feeling that way. If you wake up mopey and blue, try to figure out why, but don't deny your feelings.

Some women save special outfits for "blue" days. When they wake up feeling fat or unhappy, they drag out the red pantsuit or the green dress. Those clothes look especially well and make them feel better by just wearing them. Other women have a couple of outfits one size larger than usual so they can feel thin, rather than fat, on their bad days.

Clothes

Clothes are important in how you look and feel and have an impact on your ability to be assertive. You cannot express your feelings comfortably if your skirt or pants are too tight, if your girdle is killing you or your feet hurt. It is difficult to be assertive in a working situation if you are dressed like your teen-age daughter.

Clothing can affect you in other ways as well. Sharon Kirkman describes an encounter with a female executive: "I had a woman the other day tell me, 'I can't stand it when men make sexist comments. I just can't stand it.' She happens to be very well endowed. On that day she also happened to be wearing one of those wraparound dresses where the neckline plunges all the way down. I stopped her right there and said, 'Do they really upset you?' She said, 'Yes.' So I said, 'Then why don't you cover yourself up?' The point is, if you really don't like sexist remarks, then don't display everything so people are going to say those kinds of things. You don't have to dress either like a hag or a whore."

Improving your image of yourself means challenging a lot of the things you used to take for granted. It means asking yourself a lot of questions and thinking hard to get the answers. It means being realistic and relying on yourself.

Once you begin to practice assertions successfully in non-threatening situations, you will build confidence and a new feeling about yourself. That is the main reason for listing your assertive problems from easy to difficult. By learning to assert yourself and succeeding in minor situations, you will have more confidence in your ability to do so in more important areas of your life.

Chapter Seven
If I Say That, He'll Die

AFTER YEARS OF teaching assertiveness, Janice LaRouche has come to this conclusion: "There are always irrational words that support the kind of compliance we are talking about—unwanted compliance, undesirable compliance. When you start to really talk to someone, you inevitably find words attached to the crazy compliance. How can you challenge irrational messages?"

Ms. LaRouche and other assertiveness teachers have learned that challenging those beliefs is important if a woman is going to be able to stand up for herself and take responsbility for her actions and feelings. She explains: "If you can understand what supports your compliance, the outmoded and irrational and programmed messages that support compliant behavior, and if you challenge those messages to yourself, by yourself, where they are challengable without having to confront someone, and if you sub titute another belief system, then you are assertive."

What are some of the irrational beliefs that we

drag around with us, allowing them to affect our behavior and our feelings?

Say No!

If I say no, she won't like me anymore. Challenge that. Has it ever happened? Has anyone stopped talking to you forever because you didn't want to do something? If they did, do you really miss their friendship? Or is it more likely that they felt disappointed and possibly even angry, but not for long? Or that they might have even respected you more because you refused them?

Many of us go through life thinking that one refusal, one wrong word or false step, will end a relationship, a marriage, a parenthood. That we will be left alone, unwanted, unloved, unneeded by anyone in the world. That sounds a bit ridiculous, doesn't it? Yet how often do you think those things? Usually, we are not even conscious of doing so but, as Janice LaRouche says, if you dig, you can find them.

At her Counseling Women workshops in assertiveness, Sharon Bermon asks members to make a list of the feelings that keep them from asserting themselves. "It's always the same list, in almost the same words, with each group. There are some very basic ideas that almost all women seem to have about speaking up."

Sharon Bermon's list is one that almost anyone can recognize and identify with. It includes fears of rejection, retaliation, awful consequences, loss of control, learning the truth. When you back away from an assertion, when you are afraid to express yourself, it is usually for one of those reasons. Rejection is probably the most common one, and it comes through in a thousand different ways.

What Is Feminine?

Ms. LaRouche's associate, Penelope Russianoff, suggests that for many women, the fear is being thought unfeminine. "It would be helpful to understand that women are in a long-standing historical position of having told themselves:

'It is not feminine to think about money or to question the financial problems of the family.

'It is not feminine to get angry.

'It is not feminine to challenge the person we love about his opinions, attitudes, and beliefs.

'It is not feminine to expect other members of the family to help and share in running the household.' "

There are lots more, of course. Like other areas of assertiveness, it is necessary to know what *you* are really thinking, what you really believe and, if necessary, to challenge those thoughts and beliefs if they are making you uncomfortable or keeping you from doing or saying what you want. A lot of those beliefs contradict the two key supports of assertive behavior:

The only behavior you can control is your own.
People cannot read your mind.

Karen Flug and Judy Gold make a point of impressing those two beliefs on the women in their People in New Directions workshops. "You can't control another person's behavior, and it's a joke to think you will. On the other hand, you don't have to be destructive by not even attempting to control your own behavior. There's a middle ground, and that's what we are aiming for."

Challenging these beliefs can be threatening because it is often necessary to act on them, not just to think about them. That can be frightening, as Sandy Stark of Adelphi University admits: "It's scary and that is the basic reason people don't change. I may not like what I've got, but I know it. I know every inch of this bad space that I'm in." You have to be willing to challenge your beliefs, take some action based on your new feelings and learn to live with the results.

Let's look at some of the other fears that keep you from asserting yourself and challenge them through examples offered by assertiveness leaders.

Fear of Rejection

If I tell my husband (lover, boss) I disagree with him, he will be angry and never like me again. That sounds fairly silly just on the face of it, doesn't it? If the person you are worried about is really that dogmatic, are you sure you want to be around him anyway? What is the disagreement about? Is it something so basic he cannot forgive and forget? Are you really sure he will even remember tomorrow? Or an hour from now? Has he ever been angry with you in the past about something? For how long?

Go even further. If he is angry with you, does that mean he doesn't like you? Have you ever been angry with someone you loved and/or respected? Did you stop loving them? Why will he? Do you really think his feelings for you are so shallow, so easily undermined and destroyed? If so, why are you worrying about him at all? If he's that insecure, maybe you should look elsewhere, for someone who can accept a difference of opinion without destroying a relationship.

When you begin to see the irrationality of your beliefs, then experiment. The next time a situation develops—a discussion about politics or even the weather—and you honestly disagree, say so. See what happens. You need not make a big argument or a vicious attack. Just say what you believe and see what the results are.

If I ask my boss for a raise, I'll be fired and never find another job. There are several irrational beliefs stuck in that one simple sentence. Let's deal with them one at a time. Why will you be fired if you ask for a raise? Are you not doing a good job now? If not, then you *will* probably be fired whether you ask for a raise or not. If you think you are doing a good job, if you get through days without criticism and with additional responsibilities, then you deserve a raise. Perhaps your boss just has not thought about it. Or maybe he wants to see if you have the self-confidence to ask him.

Suppose you do get fired, not necessarily for asking for a raise. People lose jobs all the time. Others change jobs. If the economy is bad, it might take you a bit longer to find a new job but, sooner or later, you will. Being fired doesn't make you unemployable. You might lose your job for economic reasons, or because of new automation equipment or because your supervisor didn't like the way you dressed. None of that has any bearing on new employment. If you were fired because you couldn't do the job, perhaps you should try something else, or start at a lower position and work your way up.

If I don't do what people want, they won't like me. Really? Has anyone refused to do what *you* want? Do you still speak to them? Why are their needs more important than yours? Why should one refusal do that? Don't you have a right to do what you want as much as anyone else?

You can probably think of a lot more examples yourself. The important thing is to challenge them. Learn to ask yourself questions and to evaluate how realistic those fears really are. Try role-playing in your head. Put yourself in the other person's place. Will they really hate you forever or just find it temporarily inconvenient? Will people really stop speaking to you if you express your own ideas? Or might they, perhaps, be more interested in talking with you because you are now an individual with her own feelings and ideas to share?

Fear of Consequences

This is very similar to the fear of rejection. I can go further, however.

Anne has recently moved to a large city. She told her assertiveness group that she wanted to ask her mother not to write so often—her mother lived several hundred miles away and wrote almost daily. Anne felt guilty if she didn't reply to each letter, but she didn't have the time and didn't have all that much to say, She was afraid if she asked the older woman to restrict her letters, she would be very upset. The group kept asking what would happen, what her mother would do, and Anne finally blurted out; "She might disown me or stop writing altogether or stop loving me."

As soon as she said that, she started to laugh. "Of course, she won't disown me or stop loving me. And if she stops writing, I can always call. I guess I just didn't think about exactly what I expected would happen except that it would be terrible. For all I know, she may even dislike writing so often and not know how to stop herself."

What Anne was doing is called catastrophizing and it is common to us all. It is usually an unconscious process. But, if you want to, you can bring it to the forefront of your mind. Whenever you hesitate to do something, ask yourself what is preventing you. What are you afraid will happen if you go ahead?

Sharon Bermon tells the groups at her Counseling Women workshops that: "People are animals. We have a flight or fight reaction. Whenever you feel uptight or upset and want to get away, to escape, that's the time to stand and fight."

The women in the People in New Directions workshops are counseled to write out their expectations, to list everything from the worst possible catastrophe to the best possible result. Then they are told to really consider the chances of each. According to Karen Flug and Judy Gold, that exercise helps women see the irrationality of many of their fears and expectations.

Fear of Loss of Control

For many women, keeping quiet is insurance. If you cannot say anything, he will not know how angry you are. If you do speak, you'll lose control, begin to cry or scream or yell. And that would be terrible. You might never regain control of yourself again.

Here we go again! Does that sound very realistic? What is wrong with getting angry? You have a right to feel angry, particularly if you have been manipulated or abused. Anger does not have to include shouting or crying. If it does, there is nothing wrong with that either. It is much better for you to express your anger than to keep it inside. If you lose control, that's a good indication of how upset you really are. But you *can* regain control. You have surely been angry at something or someone in the past, shouted or kicked or cried about it. You were able to stop and to live without shouting or kicking or crying all the time.

Or maybe you think it would not be "nice" to get angry? Karen Flug has the answer to that: "Many women would say, 'But it isn't nice, it isn't kind, it hurts their feelings.' What in the world is kind? We need to have as much honesty in life as possible. The world is a really dishonest place, in my perception and, at least in your own little niche, you should try to make it as real as possible for yourself."

That doesn't justify violence or attacking the other person. Assertive behavior is expressing your feelings. If that momentarily includes shouting or crying, that's all right. As you gain confidence in yourself and your ability to handle situations and objections, you will find that you lose control less often. You will learn that occasional screaming and tears don't make you an impossible or even aggressive person, merely a woman who feels emotions and is not afraid to show them.

Fear of Learning the Truth

Everything in life changes, even so-called truths. There is very little that is so terrible it cannot be borne, cannot be gotten through and survived and changed. The fear of learning the truth can be dealt with in the same way you have learned to deal with the fear of consequences. What are the worst possible things that could happen? If you want to write a book and cannot find a publisher, what does that mean? That you are not a writer of books, perhaps. There may be other kinds of writing you could try. If you are living with someone and learn he no longer loves you, is that so terrible to find out? Once you get over the initial unhappiness, you'll probably prefer to find someone else who can and will love you.

You take risks when you become assertive, but that is because you feel confident of the results. Even when they do not turn out as you wish, you learn to deal with the disappointments and try again. Karen Flug explains that many women think: "What if I test it out and I take the risk and then they tell me I'm no good. What do I do then? It's better to have my secret fantasy that I'm terrific than to test it out and find out nobody liked me. I could live for forty years saying I could really have been fabulous . . ." Is that really what *you* want out of life?

Fear of Retaliation

This fear is similar to "Fear of Consequences." What will happen to me if . . .

I ask my boss for a raise?

I refuse to watch a friend's children?

I tell my husband I don't want sex?
I refuse to bake a cake for a bake sale?
I don't want to stay late at the office?
I tell the waiter my steak is too well done?
I take back merchandise that arrived broken?

Well, what will happen? Will people stop talking to you? Will you be chastised and humiliated, like Hester Prynne with her scarlet "A"?

If there is a chance of violence, then it's probably wise to do whatever is necessary not to force an issue. However, even then, you can wait until circumstances offer more protection. It is probably not a good idea to assertively tell certain groups of teen-agers playing loud music to cut it out, because the din disturbs you. The racket may be annoying, but it's not worth putting yourself in a potentially dangerous situation.

On the other hand, sending food back in a restaurant or making a civil request of another adult should not be hazardous. You need not get angry and make a scene. If the waiter doesn't want to make whatever changes are necessary, ask for the manager or the chef. Make your request civilly, without anger, but firmly.

At her Counseling Women workshop, Sharon Bermon recommends what she calls escalation when you are dealing with clerks, waiters and people in similar positions. "You explain very civilly and quietly what is wrong. 'I ordered a rare steak and this one is well done. I would like you to take it back and bring what I ordered.' If the waiter refuses, you can escalate the assertion: 'This is not the meal I ordered and I do not want to pay for something I will not eat and do not want. Please bring me my meal the way I ordered it.' If that doesn't work, you ask for the manager. When he arrives, instead of being angry, you move back a step, explaining again: 'I ordered a rare steak and this one is too well done. I would like the meal I ordered.'

"You can keep doing that until you reach the president of the corporation, if necessary. Remember, though, to begin at the simple assertion as each new person joins the discussion. That way, you give them time to respond without being attacked. Assume they want to help you until they prove they do not."

Fear of Authority Figures

Most people aren't aware of this fear, although almost all of us have people or categories of people who can push us against a wall. Among the people found on a list of authority figures are parents, doctors, public officials, and salesclerks. That's right, salesclerks, especially for women. Janice LaRouche defines the problem: "Authority figures are the persons who represent a force in your life, or who are a force in your life that represent power or influence or control. The power that person has may be real or it may be imaginary and it may be the power that you project *onto* that person who may have some power, but you have extended it and made it more than it is."

In her workshops, Ms. LaRouche has found that women are afraid to call a doctor in the middle of the night, even if they are very ill. Usually, she reports, they will wait until morning so that they don't disturb the physician, even if it means spending the night in great pain. Similarly, many women accept the valuation and criticism of salesclerks without question, allowing themselves to be put down without an argument.

"The saleswoman decides she is an expert on what makes an appropriate human being and plays into your fear that you are not; for instance, that you are the wrong shape and size because you don't fit into the store's pantyhose. I don't know how many women have been reduced to slipping out of a store because their hands are too wide or their bodies are too short or their hips are too big. You think, 'The salesgirl is a professional. She really knows what a person looks like, and I am not a person because I do not fit her standards,' " Ms. LaRouche explains.

That sounds ridiculous, but all of us have had the experience of apologizing because a dress or a pair of pants does not fit right. We feel guilty because we don't fit a standard mold or have the ideal shape. Even if your hips are too big and your bust is too small to be ideal, you are still a person with the right to be treated with dignity.

There are lots of other people to whom we give authority over ourselves, some for rational and some for irrational reasons. For example, most women hesitate to complain if an automobile-repair bill is greater than the estimate. We assume that the mechanic knew what he was doing and that his bill is one of the burdens of owning a car.

Bosses also appear high on the list of authority figures. Janice LaRouche thinks society, in general, contributes to the fear that such people inspire. "I think our society nourishes, supports the whole concept of authority. It helps to keep the system operating the way it does—a highly stratified way that helps to exploit the labor force. If you have to work, you're afraid of bosses; you're docile, sheeplike, grateful for the little crumbs they throw your way. If you feel that these people are more important or smarter or more entitled to benefits than you are, you feel powerless with them."

In the 1960s, the collective assertions of students, blacks, women and various other groups began to challenge the sacrosanct atmosphere of authority figures. Their challenges revealed a lot of holes in the traditional power structures, and made people question even top authority figures, such as leaders of government and politics. As these tumbled down from their pedestals in the wake of Vietnam and later Watergate, the country learned to look much more closely at its leaders, instead of keeping at a safe distance, a stance that often misses many flaws.

Strangers can also be perceived as authority

figures, even if they have little real authority over us as individuals. Many women hesitate to reject, disapprove or walk away from someone they have just met, even if they don't like the person. It would not be "nice"—there's that word again! The other person would feel rejected or unwanted. It is necessary to be "kind," even at the expense of their own comfort and interest.

Someone has figured out that one out of every three people you meet will not like you on sight. Of the other two, one may not care one way or the other about you and the third might become a friend. With those kinds of odds, isn't it a bit silly to expect to like everyone you come in contact with? Women often find it difficult to refuse further contact with men they know they aren't interested in seeing again. They hesitate to say how they feel.

Janice LaRouche found herself doing just that and came up with a solution that works well for her. "I think you can say, 'I think we are very different kinds of people. That's not to say that one kind is better than another kind, but I think we have different interests and different ways of relating to people. I don't think it would work out.' I think you can also say, 'My time is structured so that I have a limited amount of social time and I like to use it with very close friends. I don't make many casual friendships. As much as it might seem like fun to explore new relationships, I've just allocated time, at this point in my life, differently.'

"This often works well because you are digging into your own motives at the same time and your own true feelings. As you get to your own feelings, you find that they're really not so terrible and so rejecting. In turn, you don't feel so rejected by other people when they say, 'Listen, you're not my type.' "

Learning your own motives and feelings is an intricate part of assertiveness. It is necessary to continually question yourself, to explore how you are feeling and why and what lies behind that feeling. As you do this, you will hear the irrational thoughts and beliefs that are keeping you from asserting yourself. Once you know what they are, it is much easier to argue with yourself and work into a more realistic assessment of your problems and find a possible solution.

Everyone has her own set of irrational beliefs that she's inherited from parents, teachers, friends and relatives through years of growing up and even after. But what was once true, if it ever was, may no longer hold water. It is necessary to check each time, to listen to what you are saying to yourself, to argue with yourself if necessary and to pick up new beliefs. Those, too, may have to be discarded in time. As long as you are aware of the need to challenge and change, it will become easier to find and erase the irrational thoughts from your thinking and responses.

Chapter Eight
Hidden Aggressions

MUCH OF THE conditioning forced on women has taught them to be passive and secretive about their wants and needs. Women are not supposed to be demanding or even express their feelings aloud. Instead, they are taught to use less direct, and often less effective, ways of making requests and stating their wants.

Sandy Stark of Adelphi University points out: "Women have not had power in the world. Our power has been manipulative; it has not been straight. In other words, we do have some power, but we use it very underhandedly, very manipulatively. In becoming assertive, we're going to have to give up that manipulation. We're going to have to lay some cards on the table that we haven't laid there before. From the age of zero, women have been taught that one way of getting male attention and gifts is to look pretty. If we want something from a man, we flirt, we dress a little sexier, we do all kinds of stuff and then we, by the way, ask for what we want."

There are other passive ways that women express their feelings. Many of these ways seem compliant and even submissive on the outside but a deeper look reveals the hidden aggression behind the actions.

Forgetting. When plans are made and she is not consulted about her schedule or convenience, some women just forget. Even when it is something a woman is interested in doing, she expresses her anger by erasing the occasion from her memory. The result is, usually, more confusion and hard feelings than would have resulted had she originally said she was busy or uninterested or angry about not being asked.

Misunderstanding. A man is often incredulous when his usually intelligent wife totally confuses some simple directions or requests. She may, for example, take the wrong suit to the cleaners or show up at the wrong time and the wrong place or dress inappropriately. Frequently, the woman announces her anger by saying something that was supposed to be kept secret or at least not revealed to the person she is talking with. Invariably, her excuse is, "I'm sorry. I guess I misunderstood you." Not every case of misunderstanding is hidden aggression, of course, but when a pattern develops, it might be wise to question what you are really trying to say.

Procrastination. For many women, this seems to be the most effective method of getting back at someone who has angered them. Usually, as with almost all hidden aggressions, it causes more problems than if she had expressed her feelings in the first place. Many women justify their procrastination by thinking, "I did not want to do that and if he had asked me, I would have told him. Since he didn't ask me, but just ordered me, I won't do anything and see how he likes that." He won't like it and he'll probably be very angry. In a work situation, it could get you fired. At home, it will probably cause more arguments. If someone does not ask if you want to do something, you still have a right to tell him you dislike the task. Perhaps a compromise can be reached. If not, at least you won't feel a simmering resentment toward the work and the person who ordered it, to say nothing of your anger at yourself for not speaking up.

Chronic lateness. Comedians continually tell the stock joke about the husband waiting at a theater or restaurant for the wife who is always late. If you can't get somewhere on time, you might ask yourself if you really want to go. If you do not, if you prefer to stay home or go elsewhere, it's a lot better to say so than ruin the occasion by showing up late and leaving your escort furious. If you're always late, that could indicate you feel out-of-control and out-of-touch with your world. It might be time to re-examine what you're doing and whether you want to continue doing it.

Refusal to learn. This is a close relative of forgetting and misunderstanding. A classic example is the wife who hates to iron and always irons her husband's shirts wrong, starching the collars, which he hates, and leaving the cuffs limp when he prefers starch. It can be found in lots of other areas as well. Like the other forms of passive aggression, it is a silent and not very effective way of retaliating.

Psychosomatic illness. Ulcers, headaches, colitis and colds are frequently cited as the most common ailments resulting from psychological problems. There are many others—everything from asthma and allergies to constipation—and they also can be traced to psychological causes. Of course, not all forms of these illnesses are psychological, and often the physical symptoms appear after the original cause has disappeared. However, if you or anyone in your family is plagued by an illness that might have emotional as well as physical causes, it's not a bad idea to explore the problems that might be behind it. Bottling up anger and resentment is almost sure to lead to some kind of physical ailment. If you pride yourself on never losing your temper or showing your emotions, you might look for the other ways your feelings come out. They don't just disappear. None of us are so perfect that we never get angry.

Nervous habits. The symptoms are wide-ranging and change with situations and kinds of stress. Some people have developed speech habits, beginning every sentence with "no," or similar expressions that indicate hostility or tension. Others twist strands of hair, chew fingernails or tap a finger or foot. If you find yourself playing with a piece of thread or a slip of paper, if you hear yourself interrupting others or changing the subject, if you develop a tic or an urge to walk around, maybe you want to say something and feel restrained. Ask yourself how you are really feeling. What do you want to say? Why can't you say it? Find the irrational belief or the fear that is keeping you quiet and face up to it. Challenge it and stop pretending that you aren't bothered by something that is making you ruin a five-dollar manicure.

Nagging. Although this is a less hidden form of aggression than the others, it is also a good indicator of something going wrong. The reason for nagging may have nothing to do with the cause of the anger, but it generally indicates that the woman feels too unsure of herself to bring up the real problem. Instead, she diverts attention and relieves some of her feelings by finding another topic, one where she feels more sure of her ground.

Janice LaRouche explains: "Assertion has to do with a total sense of your rights. If you haven't got it, you've been stripped of your rights by one irrational message after another. Assertion has to do with getting rid of a whole series of irrational messages that work on behalf of the people in power, but not in your interests."

In the examples of hidden aggression above, it is clear that the person practicing the aggression, however subtly, feels uncomfortable with making a clear statement of her feelings. Instead, she chooses devious and unclear ways of expressing herself and getting rid of her anger. The results are rarely satisfying or effective. Usually, they create more resentment and bad feelings in an endless pattern. Assertiveness-training allows you to break the pattern, to speak your mind without fear of the consequences, then to resume more amicable arrangements.

Chapter Nine

The Manipulators

JANICE LaROUCHE TELLS her assertiveness groups: "You can't exploit people with a whip. You can't get people to work for no money or very little money, as women do at home and in the work market. You don't get people to do that with a whip. You do it by stripping them of their personhood. One of the ways to do it is to erase assertive qualities, the sense of self, of self-esteem, so that people feel inadequate and unable to perform at any other level."

There are many reasons why people are sensitive to manipulation and everyone is sensitive to different ploys in different degrees. In order to protect yourself against manipulation, you must first discover your own areas of sensitivity, the things that make you nervous or unsure of yourself and, therefore, vulnerable to manipulation by someone else.

What's Your Sore Point?

Sore points are radically different for different people, and not everyone is sensitive to the same degree all the time. But here is a list of areas in which you may be vulnerable to being manipulated:

Height. If someone comments on your height, either because you are very tall or very short, that frequently can throw you off. It implies that you aren't normal, that you must be less than feminine if you are tall, or less than adult if you are short.

Weight. Almost all women are sensitive about their weight, even if they have perfect figures. For example, if you want to go to an Italian restaurant and your date prefers Chinese food, he may attempt to manipulate you by reminding you that pasta and Italian bread have a lot more calories than the rice served with chop suey. If you are overweight, or think you are, you will probably allow yourself to be manipulated by his argument.

Looks. Again, women are particularly vulnerable to remarks about their appearance. The mention of wrinkles or grey hair, a comment about a large nose or a blemish can make a woman cower into a corner, wishing for a bag to put over her head. Most will go along with anything as long as it changes the topic.

Past experience. This is another area of fruitful

exploitation by the clever and aggressive manipulator. Your vulnerability is wide-open, depending on your particular feelings and past responses.

Work. Even women with careers worry about their qualifications and their ability to find another job if they should lose the one they have. Women in non-professional positions—secretary, clerk, receptionist—may feel unsure about their importance to their employer or their contribution to the office. For a woman who is not working, the problems are even greater. If she is staying home, living on income earned by someone else, she may feel she has no right to interfere in financial decisions, even if those decisions affect her life.

Background. This can be almost anything, but it usually involves family life and childhood. If you come from a poor or unsophisticated family and are now living in a radically different environment, you may be thrown when someone comments on your accent or asks where you were raised, or when your husband throws up your childhood to you during an argument.

Education. This, too, is a very common area of vulnerability. Although it is most frequently found among people who hold responsible executive positions with little or no formal training, even a Ph.D can be sensitive. At one assertiveness-training workshop, a woman said she felt unsure of herself when someone in the office began to talk about college. She had only finished high school, and, although she is very intelligent and has a high-paying job, she became nervous when the subject of higher education came up in conversation. The leader of the group, a woman with a Ph.D. in psychology, admitted that she still has nightmares about not passing her examinations, even though she had passed them years ago.

Cooking. Some women are not good cooks and do not care to learn. Others are passable cooks and would like to be better. They, in particular, react to comments about their cooking and will frequently try to get the jump on any criticism by apologizing before anyone has even tasted the food.

Athletic skill. This one probably goes back to the games of softball, tag and Red Rover in childhood. If you were always among the last to be chosen for a team, a discussion about sports or a suggestion to play may still make you nervous and insecure. All those childhood memories of standing in a dwindling group return and are added to your present lack of interest and skill.

Music. There are people in this world who are tone-deaf, without interest in or desire for music. Some have learned to live without apologizing for their lack of concern. Others find that the mention of music brings on a case of the heebie-jeebies. They feel there is something deficient in them because they cannot appreciate or even hear music the way others do. Furthermore, they feel guilty about the deficiency, convinced it is a sign of their general unworthiness. Hum a tune and they cringe, afraid they will be found out and exposed to the world.

Age. This one goes both ways. A younger person, someone in her teens or early twenties, can almost always be manipulated by bringing up her tender age. At the other end of the spectrum, it is possible to get to an older person by saying: "You don't understand. You are too old and don't know what's going on in the world."

Vocabulary. This usually goes along with a sensitivity to education, although it might exist on its own as well. Your palms and underarms get clammy whenever someone criticizes your speech or supplies you with a word you could not recall or did not know. While you wipe off your wet hands, the other person takes advantage of your nerves.

Worldliness. Sophistication or lack of it has little to do with real maturity. It is possible to understand the workings of the world in all of its intricacies and not know which wine goes with what food or how to hail a taxi. It is human to wish for what we do not have and to feel insecure when we compare ourselves with others. The idea is not to let that insecurity allow someone else to take advantage of us.

Face It Realistically

These examples can give you some idea of what you might be sensitive about. The next step is to make your own list, being very honest with yourself. Try to figure out why you're particularly vulnerable in specific areas and how realistic your sensitivity is. Does it really make you less of a person if you can't read music? Will people care if you were brought up in a poor neighborhood? Do five-syllable words say more or mean more than words of one syllable?

It may take awhile to find all your vulnerable areas and to work out your feelings about them. Probably, you will never completely rid yourself of nervousness whenever the subject is mentioned, but that doesn't mean you must remain open to manipulation.

The Great Manipulators

"People will manipulate you by using your vulnerability," explains Janice LaRouche. "Your vulnerability can be projected onto a situation, or people can manipulate you by discovering you are sensitive about something and throw you off your assertive center. Most people in our culture are highly manipulative. It's a finely honed skill. People are very good at it. They don't know how to be assertive, but they are great at manipulating."

Ms. LaRouche has devised a technique for dealing with the sensitive areas and vulnerabilities we all have. She suggests her students pick up on the manipulation, examine it, then toss it aside. It works something like this:

He "Do you really want Italian food? All that pasta and bread won't help your figure, you know."

She: "I'm very sensitive about comments on my

weight. I'm aware of my problem and won't eat pasta, but I do want Italian food."

Or take another example:

Joan is arguing with her teen-age son about his responsibilities. The boy says: "The problem is we have a generation gap."

To which Joan replies: "Yes, you're right. You don't understand me."

She has recognized what he was trying to do— make her feel nervous about her age and differing values. Instead of responding the way he expected, taking the blame herself and asking what could be done, she threw it back on him. She was not accepting the manipulation.

Recognize the Ploys

There are an infinite number of manipulative ploys that are used, sometimes by themselves, sometimes in combination with each other or with a person's particular sensitivity problems. It is often valuable to know these techniques. Knowledge makes recognition easier and defenses more effective.

Guilt. This is one of the biggies. Almost anyone can use it against anybody else, but it is most frequently found in family situations. Usually, there is a catch phrase that points out the manipulation:

"How could you do that to me?"

"You don't care about me anymore."

"You are making me unhappy."

And so forth. Get out you list of rights again and reread them. You have a right to refuse a request without feeling guilty. No one can make you feel guilty. You do that to yourself, allowing yourself to be manipulated by the other person.

Anger. This is very effective, especially against someone who doesn't feel comfortable with screaming and other aggressive behavior. When a woman refuses to act the way a man expects, he begins shouting and yelling. To end his behavior, which is aggressive and unpleasant, she gives in and agrees to his demands.

Obligation. This is in the nature of an unsigned contract. If I do this for her, she will have to do the same for me. Not necessarily, unless you both agree ahead of time. Nor do you have to return a favor if it is inconvenient or disadvantageous to you to do so.

Criticism. When the argument or discussion isn't going his way, the other person switches tactics and finds something wrong with your behavior. You rush to meet the attack, get flustered and lose your cool. Then he plows ahead with the original argument, and you have won a battle and lost the war.

Insecurity. The opposition takes unfair advantage again, but that's what manipulation is all about. By changing tactics or topics midway, you get defensive and become unsure of yourself. For example, in the middle of an argument about the family budget, your husband brings up the last meal you ruined, knowing you are sensitive about your cooking and unsure of yourself in that area. Instead of sticking to the subject, he catches you off guard. Your assertive response, of course, would be to point out that the meal, while definitely expensive and definitely ruined, has nothing to do with the topic at hand.

Inadequacy. This is similar to the "Insecurity" tactic. Your shortcomings suddenly become part of the discussion, regardless of the original subject matter. For example, by unexpectedly pointing out that you never make social arrangements, but let him make all the plans, your man puts you on the defensive. Again, the best response is a passing glance at the manipulation and a swift return to the real discussion.

Helplessness. This one is most frequently used by bosses—"It is imperative that we get this contract out today and you are the only one who knows how to do it correctly"—parents—"I'm all alone and have nowhere to turn for company except my daughter and now you don't want me"—and children—"I can't do my homework and clean up my room by myself. I need you to help me." Invalids and infants are helpless. Most of the rest of the world can cope by themselves within limits.

Teasing. This can be combined with general putdowns. It's done in a supposedly loving, affectionate way but, underneath, there's manipulation coming through. The teaser is trying to get the teasee to do something. When the teasing doesn't work, he may escalate: "What's the matter, don't you have a sense of humor?" Remember the tactic, notice the manipulation, comment if necessary, then return to the point. What does he really want?

Questions. This is most frequently used by women, but many men have learned its effectiveness. The question is usually of the "Why did you? . . ." variety. He already knows the answer and wants you to admit a mistake or a bad move. Then, having admitted your goof, you will be more likely to follow his lead. But you are entitled to make mistakes. They need not hound you for the rest of your life. If questioning is someone's pattern, answer briefly, deny the question's importance and go back to the point at hand. The question probably had little to do with the real discussion anyway.

There are other kinds of manipulations and almost all are hard to recognize when they are happening. Afterward, it's easy. You feel uncomfortable, exploited and used. When you feel that way, go back over what just happened. See if you can find the manipulation and recall how you handled it. Think of what else you could have done when the situation popped up. How would that comment of yours have ended the discussion? Would you still feel the same way? Eventually, with time and practice, you will learn to spot manipulations as they are being thrown at you. Then you can duck and let them pass overhead, or catch one and toss it aside.

Even when you learn to recognize and ignore the

manipulations, they may not stop. Some people are too ingrained in the habit. Others don't realize what they're doing.

And you may be giving out clues that you are still vulnerable to manipulation.

A Visit from Mother

As an example, let's use the impending visit from Mother. When she calls, she opens by saying she would like to stay for two weeks. You explain that you are very busy, have an almost impossible deadline to meet and there is no way you will be free to entertain her or spend any time with her on the dates she's chosen.

Mother does not give up. She brings Father to the phone who also says he wants to come to see you. Once again, you explain the deadline, the pressures, the contract you must fulfill, and the work you must do. No way, you say. I just don't have the time when you want to come.

They both point out that they will not be able to drive to your city in the winter, that they haven't seen you in months.

"Surely, you can spare some time for your parents." (Implied is the threat that they will not be around much longer to bother you—and you, heartless person, don't care.)

You continue to refuse and, finally, they get the message. They are not welcome at this time, although they will be welcome later, when you are freer.

When you hang up, you shake you head. "That's my family. Never say die. They don't give up until they run out of ammunition, no matter what the cause." What you don't realize is you gave them the signal to keep talking and asking. By blaming a deadline and work pressures, you suggested that it was not really your fault and you were not responsible for the problem. They, in turn, felt that if someone at work could control you, perhaps they could also.

The Fall Guy

"Someone, something else is the fall guy," says Janice LaRouche. "Life. You're caught up in life's circumstances and can't do it. No! You make your own decisions. The assertive person makes her decisions, establishes her priorities and then it's much clearer to others that she is not manipulable. Every time you bring in some other force, a deadline or whatever—the other thing making it impossible —you're not only giving an invitation to be manipulated on this issue, but you're also announcing that you cannot speak straight out and stick to your point."

It is not always other people who manipulate us. Sometimes we are guilty of manipulating ourselves, and that can be as disconcerting as having someone else do it to you. When you manipulate yourself, you project your assumptions about other people into a situation that might not be as anxiety-provoking as you think.

Janice LaRouche explains what occasionally happens to her: "My psychological barrier is that if I am different from other people, they will not accept me. If I'm offbeat and have my particular ideas, people with very different ideas won't accept me. So I stand up before an audience and, if I project onto the audience, read into them qualities of difference—like they're very conservative and they won't understand what I'm saying—they won't be empathetic and so on, I can fall apart and be unable to make an effective presentation. If I project onto the audience empathy and interest in my topic, alert and intelligent looks, I can just zoom with a topic and keep going and going and going. But the audience is not manipulating me. I am manipulating myself."

What Could Go Wrong?

If you begin to feel anxiety or extreme nervousness in a situation, ask yourself whether there is a real cause for your feelings. If you're on a plane being hijacked, the answer will naturally be "Yes." If you're meeting a lot of new people at a party or at some other public function the answer is probably "No." If you think that you're making yourself nervous, ask some questions.

What could go wrong? What would that mean? Will it really make a difference tomorrow? Next week? Next month? Will it affect the rest of my life or just getting a particular contract, job, man or friends? Make a real effort to see things in perspective, to acknowledge inside of you that few things can really change the course of your life unless you cooperate. Understanding and believing that will make it easier for you to be assertive and much more difficult for someone else to manipulate you.

Chapter Ten
Finding the Words

PROBABLY THE MOST difficult aspect of assertiveness is learning its language. Assertive language uses "I" statements. You express your feelings and wants and needs without reference to anyone else. Sandy Stark is thinking of calling her courses at Adelphi University "explicitness-training" because: "Our actions, our words are explicit. They are clear. They are not muddled messages. They are not vague and they are not double messages."

That does not mean that you must go around talking about yourself all the time in order to be assertive. There are many times and places when assertiveness is not a problem and should not affect what you say or do. In those situations, your language and responses should be no different from what they have always been. You may, in fact, find yourself more concerned with others and ask questions to learn how they are feeling.

When an assertive situation arises, however, it is necessary to know what kind of language to use and why you should use it. There are no real rules or points to remember, just some ideas and reactions that you should be aware of and watch for.

"I Am Furious!"

Penelope Russianoff tells about Norma, waiting for her husband, Steve, to come home. He's very late and she's been waiting for a long time. When he finally arrives, she is furious. As he opens the door, she says: "You son-of-a-bitch. You're just like your father. You take no responsibility in letting anyone know when you're coming and when you're going. And, what's more, you really don't care about me."

"That's all 'You' language and it gets you nowhere in dealing with your anger," says Dr. Russianoff. "It's much better to say: 'I am just furious. I was waiting here all evening because I thought you would be home at ten, and it's now one-thirty. I wanted to take a shower, but I was afraid I'd miss your call and I just sat here getting more and more angry, seething more and more. I really wanted to go to bed, but I was so furious that I really didn't feel like going to sleep. Besides, I didn't want to miss you when you came in. And I want you to know that, Goddamnit, I'm really furious and, next time you go out, I'm going to remind you that if you're going to be late, I really expect you to call me. This way, I'm just so angry with you that I had fantasies of sticking bolts on the door so you couldn't come in when you did come home. I don't want to act that way, but I sure feel like it.' "

As Dr. Russianoff points out, that's a much more effective way of dealing with your anger. It lets the other person know exactly how you feel and why, but it does not attack or demoralize him. You take the blame for your feelings and your actions. You point out the things that really bother you—the lateness of the hour, the lack of contact—and you offer a reminder to call the next time.

Never assume that the other person knows what you're thinking or even what you expect. There is no way he can know for sure unless you tell him, as explicitly, clearly and directly as possible.

Asking the Right Questions

Having told the other person how you feel, the next step is to learn how he feels. Again, you cannot be sure unless he tells you. Ask a question. Ask several questions until you are sure in your own mind about the feelings and expectations on the other side. When you ask questions, however, try not to be manipulative. Avoid "Why" questions. Concentrate on "How" or "What" questions. How do you feel? What do you want to do about it? How can I help you? What rules or expectations do you have? What kind would make you feel comfortable?

Once you know what is expected and wanted by others and are in touch with what you want and expect, you can begin to find a solution. In the example given above, the two people involved might reach a compromise. If either one is out after eleven o'clock, the person at home is called. Some estimate of arrival is made, some reassurance of care and interest is offered, and both can feel more comfortable.

Such solutions are not possible if the other person is put on the defensive. When you use "You" language, you almost invariably attack the other person. He or she may, in fact, have done something that leaves you distraught, but an attack on them is not going to solve the problem. It will probably make it worse. Try another tactic.

Family therapist Katherine LaPerriere explains: "You can do other things. You can ask questions of the other person. You can't go through life making "I" statements only. You can say, 'Is it important to you that we do such and such? How do you feel about this? Or what do you like about that?' That's very different from accusations."

Attacking the other person puts him or her on the defensive. If you're both busy fighting off the other's accusations, neither can think about solving the original cause of the problem. It does no good, for example, to tell your boss that you cannot finish the work because he gave it to you too late. Instead, try saying something like this:

I always work better if I have some time to think about what I will be doing and to plan what has to be done. When I get last-minute work, I feel very pressured and rushed and I end up making more mistakes. I prefer having time to do the work well.

Responsibility

The key to what you say is responsibility. You must be willing to take responsibility for your feelings and your actions. You cannot blame them on someone else. Other people cannot make you upset or hurt or even nervous. You do that to yourself. If you're angry or upset, it's okay to say so. It lets the other person know how you are feeling. It gives him a clue about how to act and what to say in return. If you are calm and matter-of-fact, he will respond in the same way. If you begin to scream and yell, he will probably answer in similar language and tone.

"I get upset when you say that" is a lot different from "You are upsetting me by saying that" and even from "It upsets me when you say that." With the first sentence, you are taking full responsibility for your feelings. You recognize that someone else may not be upset by the same statement and that it is not maliciously intended to upset you.

More "I" Statements

There are some "I" statements that are not assertive, and it is important to watch for those. They are similar to the qualifiers mentioned in chapter two:

"I don't want to sound silly, but . . ."
"I'm not sure this is important, but . . ."
"I don't know if I can help, but . . ."

"I probably don't know too much about that, but . . ."

"I may be wrong, but . . ."

Sharon Kirkman, of Boyle-Kirkman Associates, a management-consulting firm, explains her not uncommon reaction to hearing someone using such qualifiers: "When I'm dealing with a woman who says to me, 'I don't know if this is important, but . . .' and then she says what she is thinking, I guarantee, I don't think it's important either. I think that's the biggest key in assertiveness-training for women because that's what we do most often. We preface everything we say with these disclaimers. That's the biggest thing. The second thing is we talk too much. The most important people in business, in politics, in anything, are people who speak very positively."

In chapter two, it was suggested that you try to hear yourself using disclaimers and keep a record of the situation and person you use them with most often. Now is the time to take a look at that record. What are the situations that make you insecure and unsure of yourself? Did you really think something you said was unimportant or silly or unnecessary? If so, why did you say it? Keep listening to yourself. If you hear yourself using those disclaimers, those qualifiers that immediately put down your thoughts —stop. Start again without the disclaimer. You might even say: "No, I didn't mean that. I think this is very important and I would like to express myself. I think I have a solution or another way of looking at the problem."

Don't Put Yourself Down

Whatever you want to say, don't put yourself down before you say it. The person who is listening to you can only think: "If she thinks it's silly or unimportant or stupid, then I probably shouldn't even listen to it. If she doesn't think it's really worth saying, then I don't have to pay any attention to it." If you want to be taken seriously by your husband, boss, friends, even strangers, don't put yourself down before you say what you think. That is hard to do and most of us make those qualifying statements out of nervousness. So when you hear them coming out—stop! Go back and start again.

There are other problems to watch for, especially in emotional situations where it is difficult to predict how you are going to react. If you say something you don't mean or don't want to be taken seriously, you can always say so. You have a right to make a mistake, verbally or by action. You have a right to admit the mistake, do what's necessary to correct it and not be forever bound to it.

Arguments

When you are in an argument, especially with someone who is close to you—a parent, husband, lover or child—listen to yourself. If you hear the words "always" or "never," stop. Whatever the argument, it should not go into the deep dark past or project into the future. Those two words are accusations; they attack the other person—and leave you open to attack as well.

Dr. Russianoff cites an example: "If Norma says to Steve, 'You are always late. You never think about anyone but yourself,' he can answer, "You're telling me I'm always late. That's not my impression. Tonight I was late. And I remember last month I was about a half-hour late. But, usually, as I see it, I am on time.' "

"Always" and "never" are words that will get you into trouble. They will be seen as attacking words and justify the other person defending himself and attacking back. Also, they bring up the past when you should be concerned with the specifics of the present. If you said nothing in the past when someone was frequently late, why bring up that resentment now? What good can it do? What can they do to change it?

If You're So Good, Why Aren't You Married?

Sharon is thirty-three, vice president of a bank, smart, pretty and single. It's a state she has voluntarily chosen and thoroughly enjoys. She's had a number of long-lasting affairs, never lacks for dates, doesn't want marriage ever.

Although her parents have more or less become reconciled to Sharon's status as a single woman, the rest of her conventional family finds it difficult to accept. A middle-aged aunt is particularly pushy on the subject, bringing it up at every family occasion. Lately, Auntie has taken to giving Sharon's telephone number to likely marital candidates, and these are not men Sharon herself would choose. She finds she must put a stop to an increasingly annoying situation. She calls her aunt:

"You are always meddling in my life. If you don't like my being single, that's too bad. Next time you give my number to a man *you* like, or start in on me with that nonsense about marriage, I'm going to stop talking to you."

Sharon's aunt is surprised and angry. She's been talking to Sharon about getting married for a long time without a negative response. The aunt answers the attack by defending herself. She's doing it for Sharon's own good. What kind of life is it to substitute a career for the love of a good man? Although they finally part with courtesy, the family breach will be a long time healing.

Suppose Sharon had not attacked her aunt, but had said instead: "I know you want the best for me and I appreciate your concern. But it's my life and as an adult I ask you to let me lead it. Please don't give out my telephone number to men. And please stop talking to me about marriage. We disagree too strongly to discuss it and I love you too much to want to get into arguments. Let's just stop."

Assertive statements may be descriptive statements, but they are usually followed by an expression of feelings or an explanation. For example, if you say, "That statement bothers me," you should follow it up with an explanation. What is it about the statement that bothers you? How does it bother you? What would you prefer instead?

Once you've described the situation, go on to your feelings. Let the other person know that you are upset or excited, happy or angry. Then he will know how to respond most appropriately. That way, also, you keep control of the situation. He is responding to how you feel and what you want instead of setting the limits himself. If he disagrees with your feelings or feels differently about something, he has the right to say so as well. The two of you can work out a compromise.

Accentuate the Positive

Assertiveness is a middle ground between compliance and aggression. If you are usually aggressive in some situations, you may want to back down a bit, to say what you want or feel or what you are willing to do, without blaming or accusing the other person. If you are often compliant, giving in to someone else's ideas, going along with their plans, you may want to speak up for yourself. Most compliant people don't express their own feelings because they're afraid of the response. They fear that they'll be ignored or laughed at, that the other person will be angry, disappointed or bored. Finally, it is often difficult for a usually submissive woman to flat-out refuse a request or change a situation. She just doesn't feel comfortable making those demands.

There is nothing wrong with softening a request or refusal. It doesn't have to be an "I want" or "I need" statement that offers no possibility of compromise or change. Instead, use empathy and understanding. Put yourself in the place of the other person. Sandy Stark has some ideas on this tactic that she passes on to the women in her assertiveness training courses: "You start with a positive because people can hear you a lot easier when you start with some appreciation. You start with appreciating their humanness, and they can relax and hear you. If you start with something that's going to put them on edge, they may have trouble hearing you. I'm not sure every assertion had to be a confrontation. I think it can just be a statement, made with empathy and feeling. Assertion with empathy is a lovely combination."

Nicknames

Laura had never had a nickname; even as a small child, she was known as Laura. When she began working as a legal secretary, one of the lawyers in her office started calling her "Spanky." At first, she thought the name was funny—it didn't bother her. Out of curiosity, she asked the man why he'd chosen that name, and he said she reminded him of Spanky in the old *Our Gang* comedies.

Laura noticed that all the women in the office had nicknames, bestowed by the same lawyer who'd called her Spanky. The other men picked up this nickname-calling from him. On the other hand, all the males were referred to by their proper names. That bothered her. The more she thought about it, the angrier she became. She decided that she didn't want to have a nickname, certainly not Spanky, and that she would let that lawyer know. The next day, she walked into his office and closed the door.

"I am really flattered and pleased that you like me well enough to give me a nickname. I recognize that it's a sign of affection and belonging, and I'm glad you think of me that way. But I don't like nicknames and I do like my own name. I would prefer it if you called me Laura from now on."

The lawyer was surprised, but agreed. He didn't feel put down or attacked because Laura had begun by putting him at ease. By acknowledging the thought that prompted the nickname, she had actually complimented him. When she did express her objections, they were clear and direct, and the older man found them unthreatening and real. He agreed to her request. She was Laura at the office as well as elsewhere in her life.

Beginning with a softener, an empathetic statement that tells the other person you understand what he is saying, even if you disagree with it, is both effective and useful. If you are at a public meeting, for example, and you do not agree with something that has been said, you could stand up and express your point of view this way:

"I've been listening to what is going on and I'm not quite sure I understand everything. If we do such and such, will XYZ really happen? I think there's a chance of having XYZ and we should do what we can to stop it. I agree with the speaker who said XYZ would ruin the community, but I'm not sure I go along with the idea of asking for outside help."

The idea is not to turn off your listeners before you begin to speak. If you begin by saying you disagree or you think they're wrong or they don't know what they're talking about, the chances are very good that they won't listen to you. You have attacked them and put them on the defensive and, like the rest of us, they don't like being in that position.

"I Hear What You're Saying"

A more effective approach is to repeat briefly what the other person said, question the points you disagree with and state, as clearly as possible, your alternative views. That way, you're sure of some audience and some response. This technique is as effective with individuals as with a group. Some assertiveness teachers recommend using the phrases "I hear what you are saying" or "I hear that you are saying that . . ." as a way of keeping the debate open and less susceptible to misunderstanding. If you repeat what the other person said, you can be sure that you are both understanding and hearing it clearly.

Think Before You Speak

When you find yourself in a situation that calls for assertion, give yourself some time to think before you begin to speak. What do you want from the situation? What are your rights? What are the other person's rights? Is there a possibility of compromise?

While you're thinking, come up with an assertive chant that expresses your feelings and rights. Here are some examples to give you the idea:

"Please turn down the sound on your TV set. It was so loud it woke me up, and it's past midnight. Since sound carries so sharply in this house, would you set the volume lower after eleven at night?"

"I believe the figures you have are wrong. I've added them up myself and reached another total. Please look at what I've done before deciding."

"I don't like making coffee for everyone in the office each morning. It's not part of my job as office manager and I'd like to stop it. I'll share the work if everyone else pitches in. But I don't want to be the only one."

"I would like to return this sweater and get a refund. It doesn't match the skirt I have and I didn't find anything else in the store I want."

"I don't have time to take care of your kids today. It's very inconvenient today and I cannot help you. In the future, I would like more notice when you want me to watch them. I have my own work to do and it's often difficult for me to do this."

"I can't come to see you this weekend. I have other plans that are very important. I would like to see you, so perhaps we could set a date that is convenient for both of us. However, I can't make it this weekend."

In each situation, you have to find your own feelings, express them by taking responsibility for them and not allow yourself to be thrown off your assertive center. If necessary, keep repeating your statement—your assertive chant—with whatever variations are necessary. This is known as the broken record and is particularly effective with strangers. Each time the other person tries to argue, you repeat your assertion.

Play Catch

This can be varied to meet what the other person says. If they try to manipulate you, you play catch. Take the manipulation, acknowledge it, then toss it aside and repeat your assertive chant. If the argument makes some sense, you can respond with empathy and understanding ("I understand what you are saying, but . . ."). If the argument is specious, ignore it, offer another point in your own argument and repeat the chant.

If you aren't sure you understand, ask questions until you do, then repeat your chant. Use humor or acknowledgment or anything else that seems appropriate, but don't lose the point of your assertion. If a new tangent is opened, firmly refuse to be carried away ("I really don't think that has anything to do with the subject at hand, which is . . .").

When making an assertion, it's important that you keep your rights in mind. Do not allow yourself to be sidetracked or manipulated out of what you want. If that does happen, acknowledge it, then go back to your point. Take time before each response to be clear in your mind about what you want to say and how you feel, then go ahead.

Assertiveness Risks

Sharon Bermon of Counseling Women points out that there are risks in assertion, and you must be prepared to meet them. She gives an example of two women who share an office and secretary. One of the women decides she doesn't have time to answer her own phone during the day and that the secretary could easily do so. She stops at the secretary's desk and says: "Will you start answering the phone for me?" The secretary says, "No." The woman becomes angry and threatens to fire the secretary. Instead, the secretary quits. Says Ms. Bermon, "Don't ask questions unless you're really prepared for the answer."

She also has a formula for assertiveness that is used by the thousands of women she has trained. It begins with a description—"This is the third time this week you have asked me to work overtime." Next comes an explanation—"I don't want to work that much overtime." Then a limit or specification —"I don't mind working late once a week. If an emergency requires more overtime than that, I would like to be paid or get compensatory time off." Finally, suggest the consequences—"I am a much more effective worker if I don't have to stay late and worry about getting home."

Take Your Time

Learning to speak assertively and confidently takes time. It takes practice and thought to find the right words. Rehearsals and role-playing are good techniques for learning, especially in situations where you can foresee who will say what. You can practice asking for a raise or promotion, going for a job interview, returning merchandise or explaining that you want to go back to school or work. If you have spent the evening awaiting the arrival of a delayed husband, friend or lover, you can use the time to practice what you want to say to him. Instead of being accusatory, think about how to get your feelings across without causing bitterness or resentment.

In situations where you don't have advance warning or which you can't control, take your time. Stop to think before you speak. Try to keep control of your temper and your feelings. If you make a mistake, back up and start again. If you hear yourself saying more than you mean, stop and apologize if necessary. Listen to what you're saying.

Janice LaRouche has found that she rarely disagrees with someone if she really listens to what he is saying: "You try to look at the sense of the approach of the speaker; then you try to look at different aspects of it to get more depth and see how that works. Why do you have to make these big declarations about what you agree with and what you don't? That's not everything the person said. That's just a few statements to indicate how he thinks. You could spend twenty years with him and not know everything about the nuances of how he thinks. That's what communication is all about."

Chapter Eleven

Hating, and Loving, Assertively

ALMOST EVERYONE WHO teaches assertiveness courses, especially those for women only, warns of the dangers of overzealousness by the newly assertive woman. Dr. Warren Tryon of Fordham University is especially aware of the problem: "Assertion is often confused with aggression. When we try to make women assertive, some end up trying to see how shrill and abusive they can be. That's not assertive, that's aggressive. Men often get into problems, sometimes because they are subassertive, but more often because they bull their way through, yell and dominate and are basically inconsiderate."

Many people take assertiveness-training to learn to control a violent temper as well as to learn to speak up in annoying situations. Learning to feel and handle strong emotions of all kinds are very important parts of assertiveness.

Women are often afraid to express themselves because they are afraid of losing control. How terrible it would be if they began yelling at their husbands, crying in front of their bosses or throwing things in front of their children! Would it be terrible though? As with many parts of assertiveness-training, you must ask yourself questions, challenging your old beliefs and examining their basis, looking realistically at the situation and understanding the consequences of what you do. Janice LaRouche explains that the objective of assertiveness-training is: "To be able to say and do what you choose to say or do. It can be tricky and it is very different from what most people are used to doing."

Iris Fodor, who teaches psychology at New York University and assertiveness-training at the Institute of Rational Living, puts it another way: "Most people can't behave assertively. They do one of two things. Either they do too much or they don't do anything and hold it all in. And that has consequences. They hold it in and either they develop a headache or they just feel awful, depressed. If they are female, they may get hysterical. If you hold it in and deny your feelings, there may finally be an explosion. Then people really lose control."

Anger Problems

Dr. Fodor has recently been working with people who have anger problems: "There's a whole group of people who get what they want by bullying, by having tantrums, when they don't get what they want. That's what kids learn at age three, and there are people whose whole lives are essentially this. They've never learned how to be assertive, how to get what they want without having a tantrum. When they have a tantrum, they get what they want. Or when they pull a knife on someone, they get what they want. When they raise their voices, they frighten other people, particularly unassertive people who are very frightened by other people's aggressions. This is a way that works."

Aggressiveness can take many forms. Most people don't go around throwing temper tantrums whenever things go wrong unless they're encouraged to do so and find that their behavior is not only acceptable, but also rewarded. Tantrums don't necessarily mean falling on the floor screaming and kicking. Most adults have outgrown that obviously childish behavior. Instead, aggressive adults prone to tantrums take out their frustrations in other ways: they yell, criticize someone unconnected with the frustration, throw things, pout and sulk or they try to go around whoever denied them whatever they wanted.

When such behavior is reinforced, it becomes a pattern. If someone is frustrated at work and comes home to yell at the family and they quietly listen to the abuse, both the individual and the family suffer. The next time something unpleasant happens, the behavior will be repeated. If the other members of the family continue to respond without argument or disapproval, the pattern becomes entrenched. Changing it requires the cooperation of everyone. Everyone must be willing to accept responsibility for his or her own actions in originally condoning the behavior.

Don't Blame Men

Sharon Kirkman has discovered that this is often the most difficult lesson to teach the men and women who are part of her affirmative-action programs: "The first thing is to have everyone understand that we, as women, have as many biases as men have. We have biases against men, against one another and against ourselves. All of the men in the world havé not, indeed, ganged up on us and made happen to us what has happened in terms of the very strictly defined roles we're in. Because we've played a part in that. We've been a party to the whole problem and we must realize that. A lot of women don't. It's a lot easier to blame the other person for creating the problem than to say, 'I'm also a part of this.' We're not the whole problem, but we're part of it."

Ms. Kirkman and her colleagues spend at least one day with men in management positions in the corporations they work with, showing them how their biases affect working conditions and employees. Then, they spend another day with the women in the company: "If your behavior has caused what's happened before, somebody's going to have to change. Certainly, we can't go out there and tell all the men to change. We can tell them to change, but they might not. The one person we can really control is ourself. We can control ourselves if we want to, if we've got courage to look ourselves square in the eye and do it."

Assertiveness-training is the first step toward changing yourself. The first step, as Ms. Kirkman points out, is to recognize how you have contributed to the behavior of the people around you. If, for example, your husband or boss constantly yells and screams, cannot make a simple request or continue an argument without raising his voice, ask yourself why. What are you doing that encourages such behavior?

You may discover that that is how he behaves with everyone. All family members and employees live in constant terror of the raised voice and abusive language, never being exactly sure when and why it will come. But there are probably people in his life who don't see that behavior—his boss, for example, or parents or doctors or other authority figures. In those cases, he has learned to control his language and his behavior because the possible bad effects of a tantrum are greater than the immediate results. If that can be learned in some situations, it can be learned in others.

Problems Will Not Go Away

You are contributing to how people behave around you. You may not be able to control their behavior, but you can control your own. That means being less responsive to screaming. It also can mean being more responsive, not silently hoping the whole thing will blow over. It will—but, the next time the clouds gather, the storm will break again, and again, and again.

Few people are totally unassertive or unaggressive. If you can tell off the corner butcher, but not your mother-in-law, you have to learn to step down your response to the butcher and step up your reaction to your mother-in-law. If you can shout back at your husband, but cower in front of your boss, you must learn to transfer some of the feelings you have in family arguments to those at work. Or vice versa.

Temper, Temper!

Janice LaRouche has learned that developing an assertive chant and an image of self-confidence has kept her temper under control, even in the most difficult situations. "With the feeling that I'm not going to be taken advantage of, I have been able to get to the feeling that they aren't going to do me in, simply by sticking to my assertion: 'This is my place in line. The end of the line is back there.' That's my favorite one because it was such an eye-opener to me when I did it. Just by sticking with it, I never got angry. It really gives you a chance to hear the other person."

As assertiveness has become more natural to her, Ms. LaRouche has discovered many benefits that seem to appear unexpectedly: "Solutions come when you are not enraged. That's where assertions can solve a problem. You know you can stick to your point without getting sucked into terrible feelings of helplessness and rage that you then have to turn all your attention to. If you just know you can stick to your point, all of the other solutions become available to you."

The first step, then, is learning more appropriate responses to the aggressiveness of people around you. Dr. Katherine LaPerriere at the Ackerman Family Institute points out: "It doesn't help when you suddenly decide to speak your mind to come with a recital of injuries. It doesn't help to come with big things like 'You always' or 'You never' or 'I never' and that kind of stuff. At best, it only makes the other person bewildered. At worst, it makes him angry or it makes him not hear. It's better, if you know what you're about when the usual routine comes up, to say specifically what you would want to suggest for that particular time.

"The main thing, I think, is not to put the other person on the defensive, not to put him down, not to blame him if things went bad because, obviously, you worked just as hard. It doesn't make sense to blame one person for something that two were responsible for."

Your Own Anger—And Theirs

Anger comes in two ways: yours and theirs. Dealing with someone else's is easy compared to learning to control your own. Let's take the easier part first, then. When someone begins to yell and shout at you, the important thing is to calm him down before you lose your temper as well. Point out that loud voices will not solve the problem and you are willing to talk about the difficulties when he has calmed down. That gives you both some breathing space. You can even say that loud voices make you nervous and unable to respond, so shouting will definitely not help.

When the discussion comes, you should be clear on the subject. If you are not, ask questions until you know exactly what the problem is and how you fit into it. If you are accused of making a mistake and it is possibly your responsibility, take the blame, offer to investigate and take whatever action is necessary to correct it. Few mistakes are so terrible that they cannot be corrected or excused. The important thing is to acknowledge the error and your responsibility, then volunteer to do what is necessary to erase it.

If the situation involves a disagreement over what should be done—whether it is assigning work or where to go for vacation—keep your temper under control. In such a situation, your assertion is to describe how you feel and what you would like to do. If others involved have different ideas, it is their right to feel differently from you. If you disagree strongly, you can always refuse to participate. Once you have made your objections known and they have been discussed and considered, there is little more you can do.

The Shouter

In those cases where even a cooling-off period has not worked, you can repeat your earlier assertion: "I find it difficult to think or respond when there is shouting. Shouting doesn't solve anything, and I will wait until the problem can be discussed more calmly and rationally." If the shouting continues, the best response is a soft voice. It is nearly impossible to continue to yell at someone who is responding in whispers.

What happens when you are the shouter? First of all, take a couple of deep breaths, flash your Calm Scene and cool off. Apologize for your behavior. You know it is inappropriate and so does everyone else. You might as well acknowledge it and start over again. Keep in mind the problem and what you want to do about it. Find an assertive chant if that seems appropriate. As we said before, many women are afraid to speak up because they are afraid of losing control. We all have that problem at times, and acknowledging it openly is the best way to handle it when it happens to you.

It's Okay to Get Mad

For many women, the problem is *not* publicly acknowledging their anger but admitting to themselves that they are furious. Penelope Russianoff has been teaching assertiveness-training with Janice LaRouche for several years in addition to her work as a behavior therapist. She says, "Lots of times, women aren't even aware that they are angry. When they do discover their anger, they overkill and they don't know how to handle it. I think the first thing you have to do is be aware of the fact that you are angry. The next thing you have to do is find some outlet that isn't going to be destructive to you or others.

"I would recommend that you get rid of the anger. Try to dissipate some of the energy stored up in the emotion and then confront the person who made you feel that way. If it is not appropriate to confront the person, try talking it out with someone. Call a friend and ask; 'Can you come over tonight? I really want to tell you how angry I am at my boss. All I want you to do is listen while I tell you how awful he is, okay?' "

Confrontations

Dr. Russianoff adds that if you do decide to confront the person who has angered you, do so with assertive "I" language, not "You" language. "One of the big dangers is overkill. Let's say you move from compliance to assertion. In the first place, the tendency is to move from compliance to aggression—to bypass the assertion, not realizing you're doing overkill.

"It happens over and over again. It happened to me in one of the first assertiveness courses I ran. I really didn't want people to smoke. So I found myself belting out the most aggressive statements, the most moralizing statements, backed up with the most embracing scientific authority and public conscience and a bunch of stuff that was really unnecessary. I sounded like an aggressive, moralizing bitch when all I really wanted was to say: 'Look, I really don't want anybody to smoke in this room because I have trouble breathing and it will make it difficult for me. So please don't.' Period."

Similar warnings are voiced by Leonard Bachelis who teaches assertiveness courses to men and women at the Behavior Therapy Center: "A lot of people do that. They get fired up by therapy and they go home and say, 'Screw all this. I've had enough of this shit. From now on, I'm not cooking any meals. You take care of the cooking and the checkbook. I'm going out.' "

Right Now Women Are Angrier than Men

Dr. LaPerriere has found the same problem with her patients: "Right now, women are angrier than their husbands are. They are more dissatisfied, maybe because they have reason to be and partially because their expectations are much higher of what a marriage should be since a bigger piece of themselves is hooked into the marriage. They are aggressive and attacking, and the husbands don't seem to have the verbal equipment to deal with it. That doesn't mean that they don't walk out of here and afterwards the husband still makes all the decisions and the wife shuts up again. How to change that without being destructive, to be clear, direct, explicit and to the point, that's the problem."

Dr. Tryon of Fordham University worries about the same thing: "I think it is more appropriate to say, 'What are the words this person ought to come up with?' We'll worry about the fine embellishments later, but first let's learn the scales. Often, people just lack language. They don't know how to turn a person down tactfully because they've never been in that position. They've just said, 'Yes,' Yes,' 'Yes,' and those are all the words they know. They don't want to offend. To say, 'Don't worry about offending people, just offend them. They deserve it,' is inappropriate too, because who wants to be around such a person?"

There are ways of dealing with your anger assertively, minimizing the risk of becoming overly aggressive, being as unpleasant to others as they may be inappropriately aggressive to you. Some techniques have already been mentioned:

- Give yourself cooling-off time.
- Repeat your assertive chant and don't allow anger to take over.
- Acknowledge and apologize when you do temporarily lose control, then begin again.
- Get rid of your anger physically, in sports or exercise.
- Tell a friend who's not involved how you feel about someone you can't confront directly.

Say Something Good

Sandy Stark suggests another technique, one she's found especially helpful in public and private situations: "Reinforcing that which is good before you deal with the bad is an effective technique. If you reverse it, they never get to hear the good things and they have a lot of trouble hearing the bad. If you start off with the bad but you also want to say how much you like something, people become so defensive at that they don't hear you. They don't remember a day later that you said anything nice to them. You get heard a lot faster when you appreciate the humanness of the other person."

Since getting your feelings and wants heard is what you want, starting off positively makes a lot of sense. It can be used in almost any situation, from large meetings to intimate encounters between friends and lovers. Begin with something good—"I really like the idea of going on a vacation next month"—then explain your feelings—"But I think it's too cold to go to the shore. Let's go someplace where there are lots of things to do, like Washington." The idea is not to put down the other person's statements, but just to point out the possible conflicts.

How to Cope with Mistakes

Even at work, using a positive assertion can be very effective. For example, if you typed the wrong figures on a contract and your boss is furious, you can take the steam out of his anger and help yourself at the same time. "You're right, I made a very bad mistake on this contract. I did not proofread it carefully enough. I'll call the company immediately and see if we can change it. If that proves impossible, I'll let you know and perhaps we can find another solution—I am sorry for the mistake, but those things do happen; I'll be more careful the next time."

Unless your boss is a modern-day Scrooge with a perfection complex, that should excuse your mistake and get you off the hook. It may not solve the problem, but at least both he and you know it will be less likely to happen again. Responding to his anger by telling him he should have proofread the contract, too, solves nothing. He knows the ultimate responsibility is his and he is the one who will have to explain to his superiors what happened if the mistake cannot be corrected. Make it easier on him and yourself by taking your share of the blame and trying to rectify it as soon as possible.

Anger is only one emotion, and few of us go around angry with everyone all the time. But it is probably the most difficult emotion to deal with, and solving it shouldn't be attempted until you're more comfortable with assertiveness and more familiar with yourself while using it. There are levels of anger and people respond differently, creating further complexities. Like assertion, anger should be treated carefully, with small steps and less threatening situations first.

You can, as Dr. Bachelis does, practice role-playing a situation that might make you angry until you're sure you can handle it. He explains: "It's a provocative kind of role-playing. The participant won't move an inch and the person must develop skills and perseverance, which are very important in self-assertiveness. Don't be frightened off. Stay in there. Don't be put off by hearing, 'The manager will be here in a couple of hours. Why don't you come back then?' That kind of thing. Most people don't press their point home. They say, 'I'm sorry. Okay.' They are thinking, 'I can't do anything about this.' The group in an assertive workshop will say, 'No, don't do that. Think about it. Create a scene.' "

The Traditional Comforts of Being "Feminine"

Many women are afraid that assertiveness-training will change them, will make them less "feminine" and uncaring about the traditional comforts of being a woman. The women who teach assertiveness frequently find those doubts raised in their workshops and many of them have given a great deal of thought to the problem.

Sharon Kirkman has found an answer: "We don't want to take assertiveness-training and teach women how to be all these masculine things just because our society says that that's more acceptable in business or that's more acceptable in general. I say, that's not more acceptable at all. What's wrong with a person coming out humble? That's a good quality, being humble. We're all required at points to be self-sacrificing; otherwise, we'll never live together. We can't all be aggressive and all be tough and all be strong. There are so many nice things about being soft and warm and tender. Why can't we say that we would like a person who could be all those things, or whichever they could be while still being decisive and strong and responsible?"

Being assertive means being yourself, all the time, as much as possible. It means being able to say how you feel and take action to get what you want. It means recognizing that other people may feel differently or want something else. Sharon Kirkman adds, "It means something different to all of us. What we are saying is that you can take what you are, you can adjust your behavior—and really not all that much—and come out better understood than you have ever been in the past. Because it comes down to communication—assertiveness is communication."

Communication

Communicating is easy. We learn it from infancy when Mother responds to a certain note in our cry that means "Wet," or "Hungry," or "Bored." As we learn to talk, communication becomes more effective. We can now distinguish between being hungry and thirsty, cold or warm, happy or sad. As we grow older, we may learn new messages, some of which contradict the earlier learning. As women, we have learned to hide our emotions, not to tell a boyfriend or lover how we feel until he says something first. We learn not to show anger because that might not "be nice." And we learn not to show love because we might be "hurt" or rejected. Assertiveness is unlearning those messages and getting back to the basics.

At her assertiveness workshop, People in New Directions, Karen Flug says: "There's a lot of pride

179

in never being angry. There's a lot of pride in having an equilibrium in yourself. There's a lot of pride in always being liked. But is it really decent to say to someone, 'Gee, I'm surprised you get so upset about that. It never upsets me. It's such a petty little thing. I don't care if they do that to me. The guy kicked me three times. Life is like that and I'll just go clean it off and put a Band-Aid on it.'? You have to learn to help people identify pain. You have to teach them it's okay to feel this way."

"I Love You"

It's also okay to be in love and to say so. You might get hurt. Or you might find that you are loved back. No one has kept records on how many potential love affairs didn't happen because neither party had the nerve to say, "I love you." And that is an assertion—a perfect example of the "I" language of assertiveness-training.

Think about that. Assertiveness not only means being able to say you're angry or unhappy, but also being able to say you are loving and happy. Or that you want loving.

Sandy Stark, in her workshops at Adelphi University, makes a point of reminding her listeners about that: "Women get to be alone a lot. There comes a feeling of I can take care of myself. But I like it a lot when we lean on one another a little. Some women get into this stuff and forget it's okay to need someone else. They get so unused to being weak they forget the gentleness. We would like men to be more gentle; why should we want to become tough all the time? It's nice to be stroked. It's nice to be gentle. It's nice to be cared for sometimes. I think there's an assertion in asking for that, too.

"Women who get into being independent—an offshoot of assertiveness—get powerful, pushy, heady. They forget about the lovely thing that is interdependence. That's what makes relationships nice. I do depend on my boyfriend for some things. I depend on him for marvelous support. I would really not like being alone. When I start talking and everything he's hearing is how much I can take care of myself, that's not stroking him for the interdependence. I like that we depend on each other for cuddling, for those lovely things.

"I think independence is a lovely thing—knowing that, in a crunch, you can take care of yourself. In your basic life stance, you believe that. But interdependence is something to be aware of, to be cherished and not to be denied. It's very different from dependency. It's a relationship with someone else. People, in becoming independent, start to negate that stuff. I think that's sad. Love is interdependence."

Chapter Twelve
The New and Different

THE PROCESS OF learning anything new means that you are open for growth. Growth brings changes, whether you grow externally and need different clothes or grow internally and have different thoughts. Assertiveness-training is a learning experience and the result, if you really work at it, is growth and change.

In her assertiveness workshops at Adelphi University, Sandy Stark reminds people that: "It's a sense of personal readiness to try something new, to experiment, to take the risk—possibly to get a lot of benefits, possibly to fall on your face. Both are realistic possibilities. There's no guarantee that when I say something assertive and I'm feeling so good about it, you're not going to turn around and call me a stupid idiot—and never talk to me again. You may not like what I say and you have the absolute right to feel that way."

It helps to remember that assertiveness is not a guarantee. Everything will not turn out right just because you assert yourself. Nor will you get everything you want just because you have told someone what that is. But just as you have a better chance of getting the meal you want in a restaurant if you order it, you have a better chance of getting whatever else you want if you talk about it. You could let the waiter choose your dinner. If you don't give him some indication of what you feel like eating, you could easily end up with chicken when you wanted fish. You have to talk about your feelings if you want other people to respond to them.

Most non-assertive women find they can speak up for themselves in non-threatening situations after a few weeks of discussions and training. In riskier relationships, it takes more time and more training before they feel comfortable. Many worry about their new behavior. They are unsure of how to act and they don't know how others will respond to them. That is a perfectly natural feeling. Any new behavior means a change, a risk, different from what went on before.

If you've been generally unassertive for most of your life, suddenly speaking up for yourself will seem very threatening, even frightening. Up until now, you reacted passively, submissively, to what went on around you. That may not have made you happy, but it was a pattern you were used to, a behavior that others expected and could predict. You knew what would happen and so did the people around you. Now you want to change the pattern, climb out of your rut. The difficulty is that it is impossible to know what you'll find when you do so.

Family therapist Phoebe Prosky uses an analogy to explain the problem: "Every new endeavor is like skiing. The problem, when you begin to ski, is the tows. If you're a new skier and you can't stand up, you have to take this impossible rope tow, which is a difficult task for anyone. The obstacles are immense. As you get better, you can take the T-bar, which is easier and you get more support.

"I really believe life works like that. As you start out, the odds are overwhelmingly against you. There's no support, there are no precedents. Nobody's for it. Everybody expects something else and tries to push you back. That's why you have to work it out for yourself—so that your resolve is like iron. Starting out is hardest; I don't know how anybody gets beyond starting out anything."

The way to get beyond starting out has already been explained. Begin with simpler problems, with situations where you don't have heavy emotional involvement that can affect your life. Take a few steps to get used to the skis before you charge the rope tow. Even if you fall on your face, you can always pick yourself up and start again. It may seem unfair to use cabdrivers, butchers or the dry cleaner to practice on, but they're not going to know you're practicing. By using real situations and solving problems you feel fairly strongly about, you can further build your assertiveness abilities.

Building Your Confidence

Each time you're successful in asserting yourself, you'll build up your confidence to tackle situations that are more important to you. Penelope Russianoff finds that the women in the assertiveness groups she trains with Janice LaRouche learn very quickly how to introduce assertive behavior into their lives: "We get amazing feedback from people who have been in the groups just a short time. They feel it's the most significant thing that's happened to them. It's changed their lives. They really feel it's fantastic."

It may take time before you begin to feel that way. But when you finally learn that you don't have to passively accept the things that happen, that you can express your anger or your outrage, take steps to change conditions or improve your situation, events will seem much less overwhelming.

Fear of Change

Some people fear change so much, they never even try it. They think their reactions to change will always be negative, not realizing that assertiveness can change their attitudes as well. Thoughts and actions that once seemed very threatening no longer seem so bad. If you didn't ask for that promotion because you were afraid of being fired for overstepping your bounds, it means that you still find it difficult to confront your boss. It will take courage and stubbornness to get yourself into his office and explain how you feel. However, knowing that you have a right to aim higher, that if you're fired there are other jobs and that if he disagrees with you, you can always quit, will make the confrontation easier.

Underdogs and Top Dogs

It also helps to recognize and understand that the person you are confronting is probably not going to make it easier for you. If you've always agreed to his demands, gone along with his plans, quietly submitted to his requests, your sudden reversal will be surprising and unexpected. It would be wise to take that into account when you consider the risks of confrontation.

Therapist Phoebe Prosky explains further: "In the underdog-top dog situation, the underdog should not expect an iota of help from the top dog. The top dog invariably tries to make change as hard as possible. The underdog has to make his own way and fight to get equality. He should not expect any help. In fact, he should except to be hindered by the person above him. If people understood this, then a) they wouldn't waste so much of their anger against a person who they think should be helping them and b) they wouldn't stop in defeat saying, 'Well, how can I do it? You won't let me in your responsible position.' You have to make it all the way yourself against all the odds."

It can be frightening to realize that you are on your own, that you cannot depend on others for help or support. In many cases, the newly assertive woman finds that her usual source of support —husband, lover, friend—is the least likely to help her new behavior. That doesn't mean that the other person disapproves or disagrees with the changes. More likely, it indicates that changes are happening to him, too. He is equally unsure about what will happen and may be feeling as insecure and uncertain as she is.

The Student Wife

Sandy Stark has found that uncertainty and insecurity make themselves known in frequently unpredictable ways. She explains what happened to a woman in one of her groups: "Her husband rarely came home for dinner in the past. As soon as she began taking an evening course, he started showing up. Nothing was stated. He was not being assertive at all. But, all of a sudden, he was home with the behavioral cue, 'You've got to make dinner for me.' It was keeping her from doing what she wanted. She finally brought it out, saying: 'Let's talk about this. I don't think it's a coincidence that all of a sudden you are home to eat.'

"He denied it, said there was nothing to it. So she said, 'I like having you home for dinner. I enjoy it. But I have a conflict now because I've got something else I want to do and I want to talk about that. I want you to know that it's important for me to be with you but, for one hour a week, it's important to me to go to class.'

"The husband finally admitted he'd been coming home because of the course his wife was taking. He agreed to come home earlier that day so his wife could eat with him and still be free to go to school. That did not solve the long-range problems of her outside interests competing with his expectations, but it did help with the immediate difficulty."

As situations develop and problems arise, it helps to take some time to think about the difficulties as coolly and rationally as possible. Begin with your own feelings. If there were no obstacles in your way, what would you like to do? How would you like the difficulty resolved? What is the best of all possible solutions for you?

Again, without considering how other people might react, how would your solution affect them? Would it disrupt their day, their schedule, their work, their life? What might they prefer instead? Assertiveness is making every effort to get what you want without harming someone else or getting in the way of what he wants. Think about the problem again. Would your best solution hurt someone else? Would it conflict with what he wants? Is there a compromise possible?

Once you have answered those questions as realistically as possible, think about the reactions to your solution. What do you think is the worst thing that could happen? Write it down, no matter how ridiculous or irrational it looks. What else might happen? And what else besides that? Write all the possibilities from outright rejection of your suggestion—and the worst possible consequence of that —to total acceptance of your idea and the best possible result. Once again, look at your list. Draw a line across the least likely consequence.

A Room of Your Own

For example, suppose you have decided you really want some time and space to be by yourself. You love your family and like being with them, but you need time to relax and rest. You consider all the possibilities and decide that what you really want is to put a couple of old chairs and a desk in the attic and use that as your private retreat. While you're there, you don't want to be interrupted or intruded upon for at least an hour.

You decide to put the proposal to your husband, but you're not sure of what will happen. As you think about it, you become anxious and unsure of what to expect. You get out a pencil and paper and begin to list the consequences:

1) He gets furiously angry and says: "If you want to be by yourself, I'll leave you alone, forever." With that he walks out of the house never to return.

189

2) He is angry and confused. He says, "I really don't understand your need to be alone. I like being with you and I don't want to be by myself. Don't you love me anymore?"

3) He is angry, but says: "Sure, take the attic. But I'll be damned if you're going to spend one penny of my money to fix up a place where I'm not wanted."

4) He is upset and not sure what you want, but he says: "If you want a room of your own, go ahead. I'll help you carry the furniture and do whatever else needs to be done to fix up the room."

5) He is not quite sure how he feels, but understands your needs and says, "I think it's a great idea. If you need help fixing up the place, let me know. I hope I can come up to see it sometime."

The first reaction is probably unreal, but the possibility of it is what's making you anxious. Seeing it in black and white should help you recognize the irrationality and the unlikelihood of your husband acting that way. The others are more realistic possibilities, depending on the man and your relationship with him. You would now draw a line across the paper after the first possibility, then consider the other four as real alternatives.

Practice your response to each one. Write out your answers, go over them, repeat them into a tape recorder and play it back. Get your reactions down pat, being sure how you want to respond and what you want to say that will both explain your feelings and reassure his doubts. You can follow this routine with almost every assertive situation that develops slowly or that includes a risk of some magnitude.

Everything Can't Go Wrong

The idea is to think more rationally, to plan more realistically for your needs. If you've been hesitant before to express what you wanted or how you felt about something or someone, it was probably because you were unsure of the reaction and expected the worst possible results, no matter what you did. While it is unreasonable to expect everything to work exactly the way you would wish, it is equally unreasonable to expect everything to go wrong. That only happens to the little character in the *Li'l Abner* comic strip who walks around followed by a black cloud.

Many people have dragged through childhood and early adulthood an exaggerated sense of their personal influence. They become nervous when they're happy and their life is pleasant; they're afraid their good feelings will be a jinx and make things go wrong. They need problems in their lives, preferably minor problems, to keep the big ones away. There is a feeling, barely acknowledged, that they could somehow control nebulous forces that could change their lives. By acknowledging difficulties and denying happiness, they can keep the powers-of-disaster at bay. That way, even if they're not totally happy, at least they won't be devastated by a major catastrophe.

If you stop to think about it, that is a very silly way to go through life. Most of the disasters that befall us are unplanned and uncontrolled, and have no connection to matters of good fortune. Losing a job has nothing to do with getting a new lover. Nor does the departure of a husband or the death of a parent have any effect on whether or not you get a raise.

Crises

Gailann Bruen tries to reassure her assertiveness pupils by explaining: "A crisis is a time for growth. It can go either way. It can either serve as a teachable moment for growth or show you there isn't anything in a particular relationship. But, either way, it's extremely threatening, very anxiety-provoking for everybody involved."

Anxiety and You

Anxiety creates nervousness, fear of the unknown and fear of yourself in unknown situations. If your life begins to change drastically, through death or divorce or even through a household move, you become unsure of yourself. The props that supported you, the people you have leaned on and the expectations that you lived by have changed. Things are different, and you are insecure and unsure of yourself.

It should relieve your anxiety and nervousness to make a realistic appraisal of the effects of your actions. Once you have some idea of what may happen, you can decide whether you want to go ahead or not. Be sure that your analysis is realistic and takes into account both the worst and the best possible consequences. Then try to anticipate the most likely result. That is the one you should use to make your decision.

Once you've decided to go through with your assertion, you should keep in touch with your own feelings. The nervousness may lighten, but it will probably not disappear. There is no reason why it should. You are going to do something different. There is no way of knowing for sure how it will turn out. There is no way of knowing how you will react or how the other person will react. Nervousness and uncertainty are perfectly natural under these circumstances. The important thing is not to allow your fear of the unknown to stop you.

At their People in New Directions workshops, Karen Flug and Judy Gold try to help their clients by explaining the feelings they will be experiencing, analyzing the reasons for those emotions and finding a way around them. Ms. Flug explains: "It's the ambivalence in yourself. You haven't sorted out the issues, you haven't sorted out the pros, the cons. What's going to happen if I do this? What's going to happen if I do that? What are the consequences? You have to go back and you have to really deal with that. Then you know what to say. It's much easier to learn behavior that way. You've got to know what the questions are before you start changing. If the person isn't clear about what she wants, she's not going to go out and do it."

What If You Don't Change?

One way to get over your fear of change is to consider what will happen is you do *not* change. You can be fairly sure that life will continue as it has been. You will remain unhappy, uncomfortable, discontented or however else you now feel. The good parts of your life will probably go on as well or they may deteriorate. The situations that make you unhappy or tense will probably continue. They could easily get worse. Your frustrations could boil over, leading you to say or do something you don't mean.

Almost everyone who teaches an assertiveness course has a story about someone who made drastic changes in her life while taking the course. Invariably, the woman was very unhappy and unsure of how to go about improving things. The course gave her some ideas, some confidence in herself, some understanding that if things did not turn out well, at least a change would make them different. Most women reasoned that since they were unhappy with the status quo, any change would result in an improvement.

Liking Yourself Better

Sandy Stark has helped women in her assertive-ness-training workshops come to grips with changes in their lives.

"They go through a period of wanting to regress and go back to the way it was," she says of women whose husbands left them. "They are also saying, 'Wait a minute, I like me better this way.' There's a conflict because she liked her man better when she was the old way, but she likes *herself* better this new way. It seems that assertiveness is irreversible. Once you have begun it, you cannot deny that you have been able to assert yourself. It's like once a man has cried, he can never deny that he can cry again. It's irreversible learning, even if you never do it again. You know that you can do it. It's very powerful."

Although positive responses to assertion are far more prevalent than negative ones, you have to be prepared to face all the consequences of the "new you." Even if the people in your life don't understand why you're behaving differently or how differently you feel, they do notice the changes. Some may make them uncomfortable or unhappy for a while. Gailann Bruen points out: "It changes the balance of relationships. While that can be very beneficial to the person involved, it can also be very threatening." If you feel your new behavior is threatening a relationship you want to keep going, talk it out. That's one of the things assertiveness helps you do.

In their book on assertiveness-training, *Your Perfect Right,* Drs. Robert Alberti and Michael Emmons point out some of the common adverse reactions to assertive behavior. These usually indicate that the other person feels threatened or defensive.

Backbiting. This is most likely to happen with strangers, especially the person you told to go to the back of the line. They will make general criticisms of you without specifically addressing you. The best response is to ignore what they're saying.

Aggression. The other person begins to yell or might even start pushing or hitting you. Whatever you said is very upsetting, and the best thing is to give him time to cool off. If he's very angry and potentially violent, leave. If the discussion remains unfinished, try again later when he has had some time to think.

Temper tantrum. This is similar to outright aggression, but has a less adult quality to it. Still, the best thing for you is to give the other person time to cool off and regain control. If you try to reason with him immediately, he will probably try to manipulate you into doing what he wants. Most likely, he is just so used to getting his own way, any show of opposition or defiance, no matter how justified, will throw him. Give him time to get used to the idea.

Psychosomatic reaction. For some people, the

threat of opposition or disagreement brings on physical illness. Try to be sympathetic, but firm. This is as manipulative and immature as the other responses, but probably engenders more sympathy. Giving in to it solves nothing and will probably mean another longer struggle later. Offer an aspirin, but stand firm on your assertion.

Overapologizing. Occasionally, your newly assertive behavior will bring light to someone previously difficult and aggressive. He will apologize profusely for his past behavior and apologize even more for his present opposition. Or you may assert yourself with someone who is normally compliant to just about anyone. In either case, try to cut off the apologies. If possible, in the future, you may help him learn assertiveness.

Revenge. Some people just don't like to be crossed. When that happens, they try to get back at whoever opposed them. If that happens to you, be assertive. Confront the person with whatever you discover he is doing. Tell him you don't like it. Offer to discuss your problems and try to find a workable compromise for both. If that doesn't stop his petty taunts, ignore him.

Once you have learned to recognize these reactions and have practiced responding to them, you will feel less fearful of asserting yourself. You will have learned not only how to control your own behavior in situations, but also how to answer potentially threatening problems calmly and without anxiety. Each time you do so will make the next time less threatening and easier. You are learning to take charge of your life, to have some influence on how events work out and what happens to you.

The Older Woman

Older women usually reject assertiveness-training by arguing that they are too old and cannot possibly change their behavior after so many years. They are afraid to take the risk, afraid to learn what might happen, afraid to give up the behavior that has allowed them to survive, even if unhappily, for this long.

In his experiments at Fordham University, Dr. Warren Tryon discovered that age need not deter any woman from learning new behavior. But she must be willing to keep at it, to keep going in the face of failures, because it will not be easy. "What might take a twenty-year-old woman a month to get right, may take a fifty-year-old woman six months to get right, simply because she has been doing it differently for thirty years longer than the younger woman has. She has to learn one step at a time. She should realize that simply because she has lived longer, she has a lot more to go back on. In the end, she may not get as far as the twenty-year-old, but the shorter movement may still indicate a great change."

Chapter Thirteen

The Right Time and Place

NO MATTER HOW well you have learned the lessons of assertiveness, no matter how long you practice your assertions, no matter how carefully you choose your language, there are times and places when assertiveness will not work. In some cases, assertiveness or lack of it is not the problem—the situations and timing are wrong. The final goal in becoming assertive is knowing where and when and with whom your new behavior will be effective.

There will be times when you will be assertive in an inappropriate place or situation. There will be other times when your assertion is appropriate, but the response is wrong. In those instances when assertion does not work, the best you can do is learn from your mistake. Next time, choose the situation more carefully. Or practice more. Learn to accept the fact that you will not always get what you want, no matter how well you assert yourself.

There are some problem areas you can be aware of in advance. There are some techniques that can help you when you find yourself in difficulties. There are some situations where an assertive response might make you feel better, but do you harm in the long run.

Timing

Iris Fodor draws on her experience as a professor of psychology at New York University and as a leader of assertiveness-training at the Institute for Rational Living. She says: "Timing is important. People tend to harp on things. People are just so pleased that they've made their point, they just keep harping on it, and that drives the people around them totally wild. That's the sort of thing one needs to learn. You've made your point. Okay."

That lesson goes beyond assertion, of course. Having made your point, used your arguments and received your answer, drop it. If the subject is important to you and the answer is negative, try again another day. If not, forget it. Going around proclaiming your victory or defeat is boring to those not involved and hostile to the person who is.

Some situations require frequent repetitions of assertion over a period of time. In those instances —asking the family to participate more in housekeeping chores—keep in mind the differences between nagging and asserting yourself. Nagging is uncomfortable and leaves a lot of bitter feelings. If it accomplishes anything, it is usually the result of negative reinforcement. People will do what you want just to get you to shut up.

Assertiveness is different. You have outlined your wants and needs and expectations. You have also explained the consequences. If the kids don't make their own beds, they will not be made. If your husband does not gather up his own dirty laundry, it will not be washed. If a blouse or shirt needs to be ironed, the wearer will have to do it. Then, everyone can make his own decisions.

Dr. Warren Tryon of Fordham University explains the dynamics of learning new behavior that varies from previous actions: "When you have let a process run on for long periods of time, it's generally more intractable. It's like catching cancer in its terminal stages. You've caught it at a point where there is no return. I would expect some people have lived just long enough under certain conditions not to be able to go back."

Other People

It helps to keep in mind what effect your assertion has on other people. If you ask your boss for a raise and a promotion, and he gives them to you, it is to his benefit to make the change easier for you. It will help him support you in your new position, to teach you what is required and to look at mistakes as part of the learning process.

On the other hand, if you are the boss and one of your subordinates continually comes in late and you tell him to stop or be fired, the response is likely to be quite different. It is obviously more convenient for this person to come to work when it suits him, not you. He may therefore be defensive, aggressive or even ignore you. You must remain firm in your assertion, make clear that any lateness must be a onetime emergency measure and that if the situation doesn't clear up, if the late arrivals continue, you will fire him.

Dr. Tryon explains further: "When you are trying to shift an existing behavior pattern, it's like trying to shift the wingspan of a species. It has to be done little by little. You wait until a favorable variation occurs, reinforce that, make that occur more often and gradually you get a shift. People want changes BANG!, right now. They don't really want to sit down and shape behavior. They don't want to have it evolve over a period of time. They want it on command, right then and there. Which, of course, has the assumption that people are like computers. If I want to add and subtract things from one to another, I just put in another card and it goes through the subtraction procedure nicely and consistently. People just don't work that way. You can't push buttons and have them operate differently, particularly if they've had a long time of different behavior."

Looking at the same problem from a different point of view, Judy Gold of People in New Directions says very much the same thing: "I think with a personal issue there is a great deal of repetition that needs to be done. You're sick of running the house and having a full-time job; yet this was the pattern you started with your husband. It takes longer to tell him you want a change. In a home situation, in personal situations with friends, you can't expect to say, 'I'm not always going to do the things you're asking me to do.'

"With a boss, it is much more reality-oriented. The company may not hear you the first time or the second or the third or even the fourth; but once it changes, your firm will pay you to be different, so it will be more supportive. In a personal situation, the degree of emotion involved goes back and forth, depending on the days and issues and other things established in the relationship."

There are other differences between business and personal assertions. Assertive responses that may be okay in a personal situation can be harmful in a business relationship. Take, for example, the subject of sexist remarks.

Street Comments

Pamela went to work every day along the same route, walking two blocks to the subway. Almost daily, she passed a well-dressed, conservative-looking older man walking toward her. Every time he saw her, he would grin and say, "Terrific tits." After several weeks of this, Pamela found she was getting upset even before she left her apartment. By the time the man actually made his comment, she would be shaking with anger. She decided to say something and, the next time it happened, she turned and followed him.

"I don't like hearing that," she said to the obviously surprised man. "I'm much more a person than I am a pair of tits. If you think that, fine. But I just want you to know that I know what you're saying to me and I don't want to hear it."

The man was shaken and said nothing. The next day, Pamela noticed him walking down the other side of the street.

Pamela was able to assert herself successfully because the man was someone she saw regularly, even if she didn't know him. In other instances of sexist remarks on the street, being assertive will probably not accomplish much and may even get you into trouble. Use your judgment; most often, the decision should be to ignore the comment and keep going.

If you work in an office where someone frequently makes such comments to you, assertion may be more successful. Try not to be aggressive or openly hostile, although it's okay to tell him you don't like his comments. This should have some effect on someone you work with and see daily. Saying the same thing to a stranger on the street might frighten him briefly—or it might make him more aggressive toward you—but it probably won't stop the remarks.

There are other times when it pays not to hear or respond to a remark that you consider sexist or insulting. Sharon Kirkman tells the following story to the women executives she coaches in assertiveness-training.

What a Pretty Dress

A woman was made vice president of a big company. She was attending her first board meeting in her new position and, while waiting for the meeting to begin, was talking to two other vice presidents, both men. One was head of marketing, the other head of operations. Her new title made her vice president of sales.

The president of the company joined the group, turned to the man in charge of operations and said, "I understand we have that problem solved in North Carolina." The man agreed. The president then turned to the other two people and said, "I saw the marketing figures and they really look terrific. Gee, Jane, that's a pretty dress."

Ms. Kirkman runs through the alternatives. "Jane cannot insult him. She cannot be aggressive. She has just taken a new job and she wants to assert herself. It was a sexist remark, as nice as it was. It was also a compliment. We're not trying to go around teaching everyone to be impolite. But she has to do something. The appropriate response would be, 'Thank you very much. The sales are up in the Midwest. I'll have the figures for you later.'"

When situations are not that sticky or the person who makes a comment is not so important to your career or your life, you could be more assertive if you find the remark really bothers you.

Sharon Kirkman often finds herself in such a situation and has worked out several ways of handling the problem. "I had one the other day. I gave a speech and, afterwards, a man came up and said to me, 'Gee, the picture in the brochure doesn't do you any justice.' I'd been talking about a very serious subject for a very long time and what my picture looked like didn't have to do with anything. I said to him, 'Rather than focusing on my picture, what did you think of my speech?'

"In a similar situation, you could say, 'I don't see that my legs have anything to do with getting the job done; how about? . . .' It's important that you don't box in the other person, don't insult him, don't press him, don't throw your gauntlet out. Because if you do, you'll get it right back in your face."

Who Pays the Bill?

There are other instances when being assertive in a particular situation is just not the best solution. One woman, who has been teaching assertiveness-training for a long time, explains how she learned that lesson. She was dating a man who had been raised in Europe. When they first went out to dinner, she offered, as she always did, to pay her half of the check. He was highly offended and refused. She realized that if she wanted to continue seeing him, and she did, that she could not insist on paying her own way in restaurants. It was something that he felt very strongly about and could not give up.

She decided to come up with another solution. She'd buy tickets for the theater or a concert and he'd pay for dinner. She is an ardent feminist and, eventually, the relationship became close enough so that she could explain her feelings. He agreed that she could pay for dinner on casual dates. But for important occasions and celebrations that they shared, he insisted on taking the entire check. She felt the relationship was worth the compromise.

The Art of Compromise

Learning how and when to compromise is a difficult part of assertion. For non-assertive women, compromise or total submission is a part of life. For the assertive woman, it can be a technique to make things run more smoothly, to give relationships a chance to grow or opportunities a chance to develop. Most women find it easy to compromise on most issues. The difficulty is knowing when a compromise is necessary and when to hold out for what you want.

Iris Fodor explains that women see such situations differently than men do and are often more willing to compromise on unimportant issues. "People have to stop thinking of these things as encounters for power. Men do see these more frequently as power encounters than women. One of the reasons women give in more is that it's less important to them, that they win their point. But if you give in so often that you begin hating yourself, it can be a problem."

Stay in Touch with Your Feelings

Assertiveness should make you more comfortable with yourself and others more comfortable to be around you. If you aren't feeling comfortable or good after an encounter, ask yourself why not. It's important to stay in touch with your feelings, to continually challenge your thinking and beliefs, to go over situations so you understand why something didn't work. Just learning the language and techniques of assertive behavior will not help. You must constantly keep after yourself, thinking and reworking your ideas and beliefs to meet new situations.

It helps, also, to take into account the time and place of your assertion. The office Christmas party may seem a good time to ask for a raise, the boss being in a happy mood and pleased with everyone around him. But you will be interrupting his pleasure with business. It would also be inappropriate to approach him when there are others around. Wait for a moment when he is alone. Try to find a time when you have been particularly efficient or beneficial to the company.

In the same way, it doesn't help to approach your husband when he comes home exhausted and frustrated from work. Wait until his mood is better and more receptive to new ideas. Just as you respond more readily to assertiveness-training if you are relaxed, he will be more interested in what you are saying if he is relaxed and at ease.

Sometimes, that is not possible. If your friend calls at the last minute to announce she has to be at the hairstylist and she knows you won't mind looking after her kids for two hours, you obviously cannot wait until she is more relaxed. If it is no inconvenience to care for the children that day, do so. But when she comes to pick them up, inform her that you want more notice the next time. In other words, if you really feel imposed upon, make clear the limits you want. If that day is inconvenient, refuse her immediately without guilt.

"I Wish I'd Said That"

One of the best things about assertiveness is that you will no longer think "I wish I'd said . . ." after an encounter. You have learned to speak up about how you feel and what you want at the time you need to do so. There will be times, of course, when you will want to go back and try again.

If that is not possible, go over the scene in your head, work out what you would have liked to say and why you didn't say it. The next time something similar happens, you should be better prepared.

Planning and preparation are important to an assertive woman. For one thing, she can protect herself to a great extent against being taken by surprise. She can learn to predict responses and work out her own answers so she can stay on her point and say what she wants. For another, she is more at ease with others because she is not dreading a change in subject or an attack. She is more self-confident because she has some idea of what to expect and knows she can handle whatever comes her way.

Plan Your Goals

Gailann Bruen emphasizes the need for preparation in the assertiveness-training workshops she conducts for professional women's groups: "When I teach assertiveness to women in business, I talk about what men do. From the beginning, men are taught to think in terms of what they are going to do next. They are always planning the next step. They know the importance of having short-term, intermediate and long-range goals. I see assertiveness as taking the initiative and not waiting for people either to do for you or to you. It's particularly important in business to tell people—the right people—you have ambitions. When you do a good job, you should be sure that the right people are aware of it. You should develop a network, like men do, of outside-the-job contacts. All that's assertiveness."

The Business World

There is no question that assertiveness is very effective and important in the business world. Although assertiveness-training has gained attention through the women's movement, it has also been taken up by the corporate establishment. Most of the psychologists and career counselors who have developed assertiveness-training courses have programs appropriate for workshops in a business.

Businesswomen who have learned assertiveness find that some of the minor difficulties of work life seem to disappear. For example, as women have reached positions of responsibility, they frequently find themselves lunching with a man as part of a business deal. Most businesswomen expect to pay the check when they have invited a man to join them, but few waiters seem to understand this. An assertive woman recognizes that the waiter will most likely put the check near her male guest and she reacts accordingly, with humor. When the waiter arrives with the bill, she simply says, "This is my treat" or "We'll let my company take care of it this time."

Even in more intimate situations, assertiveness can solve problems if you plan ahead. Sandy Stark teaches assertiveness, yet men are not put off by her behavior. When she goes out with someone new, she makes it clear before he leaves her apartment that she expects to pay her half of the meal. "With a new guy, if he suggests dinner, I have to say, 'Where do you want to go? I have this much money to spend.' He says, 'No, it's on me.' And I say, 'I prefer to go Dutch.' Before we go, he knows. That way, there's no awkward moment. And he's not looking at the menu to get something cheap for himself so he can buy dinner for both of us. He's free to buy a nice dinner for himself."

Sharon Kirkman, who has taught assertiveness to women in corporate suites and factory assembly lines across the country, has her own way of defining it:

"The best that assertive behavior can do is help you communicate so you feel more comfortable. Assertive behavior helps you be more successful in business. You can be the most brilliant person in the world and, if you're incapable of communicating it, you're not going to be successful. Assertiveness is just a means of communicating your ideas and yourself. That is going to be very effective with some people, even though total communication can never be achieved."

That, in essence, is assertive behavior—being able to know how you feel and being able to communicate those feelings to others while respecting their right to feel differently. It will not always be successful, and you will not always get what you want. But you certainly have a better chance of fulfilling your needs if others are aware of them.

When things don't work out, the assertive woman looks forward to the next try. You will feel better about yourself and your place in the world. That should be worth the effort it takes to achieve.

Bibliography

Alberti, Robert, and Emmons, Michael. *Your Perfect Right*. San Luis Obispo, Calif.: Impact Press, 1970.

————. *Stand Up, Speak Out, Talk Back!*, New York: Pocket Books, 1975.

Baeh, George, and Goldberg, Herb. *Creative Aggression: The Art of Assertive Living*. New York: Avon Books, 1974.

Berne, Eric, M.D. *Games People Play*. New York: Grove Press, 1964.

Bloom, Lynn; Coburn, Karen; and Pearlman, Joan. *The New Assertive Woman*. New York: Delacourt Press, 1975.

Broverman, Broverman, Clarkson, Rosenkrantz, and Vogel. 1970. "Sex-Role Stereotypes and Clinical Judgments of Mental Health." *Journal of Consulting and Clinical Psychology* 34 (1): 1-7.

Chesler, Phyllis. *Women and Madness*. New York: Avon Books, 1972.

De Beauvoir, Simone. *The Second Sex*. New York: Alfred A. Knopf, 1952.

Deutsch, Helene. *The Psychology of Women, Vol. I,* New York: Grune & Stratton, 1944.

————. *The Psychology of Women, Vol. II.* New York: Grune & Stratton, 1945.

Ellis, Albert, and Harper, Robert. *A New Guide to Rational Living.* Englewood Cliffs, N.J.: Prentice-Hall. Wilshire Book Company edition, 1975.

Friedan, Betty. *The Feminine Mystique.* New York: Dell Publishing Co., 1964.

Harris, Thomas. *I'm OK, You're OK.* New York: Avon Books, 1967.

Jakubowski-Spector, Patricia. "Self-Assertive Training Procedures for Women." In *Psychotherapy for Women: Treatment Toward Equality.* Edited by Carter and Rawlings. Springfield, Ill.: Charles C. Thomas, Publisher, 1975.

May, Rollo. *Love and Will.* New York: W. W. Norton and Company, 1969.

Newman, Mildred, and Berkowitz, Bernard, with Owen, Jean, *How to Be Your Own Best Friend.* New York: Ballantine Books, 1971.

Phelps, Stanless, and Austin, Nancy. *The Assertive Woman.* San Luis Obispo, Calif.: Impact Press, 1975.

Rogers, Carl. *On Becoming a Person.* Boston: Houghton Mifflin Company, 1961.

Simon, Ruth Bluestone. *Relax and Stretch.* New York: Collier Books, 1975.

Smith, Manuel, *When I Say No, I Feel Guilty.* New York: Dial Press, 1975.

Steiner, Claude. *Scripts People Live By.* New York: Grove Press, 1974.